Advanced Psychodiagnostic Interpretation of the Bender Gestalt Test

Advanced Psychodiagnostic Interpretation of the Bender Gestalt Test

ADULTS AND CHILDREN

Norman Reichenberg
and
Alan J. Raphael

Foreword by Chris Piotrowski

New York
Westport, Connecticut
London

Library of Congress Cataloging-in-Publication Data

Reichenberg, Norman.
   Advanced psychodiagnostic interpretation of the Bender Gestalt test : adults and children / Norman Reichenberg and Alan J. Raphael ; foreword by Chris Piotrowski.
      p.   cm.
   Includes bibliographical references and index.
   ISBN 0-275-94163-9 (alk. paper)
   1. Bender-Gestalt Test.   I. Raphael, Alan J.   II. Title.
   [DNLM: 1. Bender-Gestalt Test.   WM 145 R351a]
   RC473.B46R45   1992
   155.2'84—dc20
   DNLM/DLC
   for Library of Congress   91-37456

British Library Cataloguing in Publication Data is available.

Library of Congress Catalog Card Number: 91-37456
ISBN: 0-275-94163-9

First published in 1992

Praeger Publishers, One Madison Avenue, New York, NY 10010
An imprint of Greenwood Publishing Group, Inc.

Printed in the United States of America

The paper used in this book complies with the Permanent Paper Standard issued by the National Information Standards Organization (Z39.48-1984).

10 9 8 7 6 5 4 3 2 1

In Memory of Raymond Bortner, Ph.D.

Contents

Illustrations

TABLES

Foreword

The Visual Motor Gestalt Test, known to most clinicians as the "Bender Gestalt Test" or "Bender," has had an interesting and long history as an indispensable clinical assessment tool for practitioners in the mental health field. Indeed, in my series of surveys on psychological test usage over the past fifteen years, the Bender Gestalt has ranked among the top ten tests across a variety of settings and population groups and has steadfastly remained an essential component of the standard test battery. However, the test's potential use has been largely untapped to date. The present volume provides the user with a dynamic method of personality screening.

Over the past fifty years, the Bender Gestalt Test has served as a perceptual-motor measure (primarily with children), neuropsychological screening device, appraisal for cognitive integrity, and as a personality test. In *Advanced Psychodiagnostic Interpretation of the Bender Gestalt Test: Adults and Children*, the authors provide the clinician with an insightful and unique approach for the Bender Gestalt based on a dynamic projective interpretive system. This contemporary approach affords the clinician a quick-screening assessment of personality via the nine Bender designs individually, and the protocol as a whole. The authors, in Chapters 3 to 11, present the interpretive foundations for each drawing and focus on the clinical features of each card. Case-study examples are offered so as to draw meaningful implications for the practitioner. In addition, review questions conclude each of these chapters. In my opinion, this is an outstanding addition to the presentation of the text as it challenges the reader to expound on detailed descriptions of the Bender drawings and formulate strategies for clinical interpretation.

The authors also give a sound introductory background to the test that includes both the assets and limitations of this novel assessment technique. Moreover, they provide the reader with a thorough overview for administration of the test and an enlightening discussion of the relationships among the Bender drawings. I found this chapter most instructive. The final section covers pertinent recent research on the test and the authors succinctly express their view that neither the Bender Gestalt nor any other one test should be the sole basis for diagnosis or clinical decision making. The Bender is most meaningful when used within the framework of a psychological test battery.

In essence, this volume provides specific and detailed clinical insights for the interpretation of personality by the Bender Gestalt Test. In this regard, the authors present an approach that taps the rich, projective material inherent in a Bender protocol. I highly recommend this text to both seasoned clinicians and aspiring students.

Chris Piotrowski, M.A.
Research Consultant
University of West Florida

Preface

This book elaborates a pan-theoretical projective personality interpretative system for the Bender Gestalt Visual Motor Designs developed over many years of clinical experience. Always impressed with the power of an individual's unconscious or inner world, we utilized our observations, derived from over twenty thousand evaluations, to develop this text. An objective scoring system based on our interpretations is currently in the process of scientific validation by nonpartisan, academic researchers, and is discussed in detail in Chapter 13 and Appendixes I, II, and III. Earlier interpretative systems for the Bender Gestalt Test (BGT) have been criticized for being too expansive for such a quickly administered test. The present volume focuses on the technical aspects of personality assessment restricting lengthy discussions of multiple theoretical foundations.

Assessment and treatment of symbolic representation of unconscious conflicts is one of the mainstays of clinical practice in psychology, school psychology, psychiatry, and clinical social work. Our system addresses itself to those clinicians with a desire to increase their skill in assessing the personality configurations of their patients or clients in diverse settings, including but not limited to inpatient medical and psychiatric hospitals, outpatient private practices and mental health clinics, university counseling centers, public and private school assessment programs, corporate personnel screening programs, various legal settings, and residential treatment programs.

Whether an experienced clinician, a neophyte student, or somewhere in between, the reader will quickly realize that our approach is not bound to any one theory or school of thought; it is basically eclectic or pan-theoretical in practice. It is based on an understanding of human behavior deeply rooted in the works of many earlier theoreticians, evolving through some one hundred years of psychodynamic thinking.

Earlier attempts to utilize the Bender Gestalt Test as a personality measure launched the test into national prominence in the 1940s. Our approach tends to chart a different course than these previous attempts. It should be noted, however, that we are deeply indebted to the brilliant efforts of doctors Wertheimer, Bender, Hutt, and Koppitz, whose works kept this test alive and well for over fifty years.

As expected, simply reading this book will not suffice as preparation for the expansive application of the test itself. The questions at the end of each chapter are designed to help readers assess their comprehension of the main criteria for interpreting each design. The subtle, rich clinical material can only be obtained through repetitious use and deep appreciation of the symbolic connotations of the human unconscious. Of course, qualification for using this test does not come from mastering this system, but from the assessment courses in appropriate graduate and postgraduate training programs, as well as years of experience.

This book is dedicated to Raymond Bortner, Ph.D., without whose guidance and instruction this work would never have been written. We are also indebted to our respective patients, whose willingness to undergo psychological evaluations permitted us to develop a cogent interpretative system to measure unconscious processes.

Without the guidance of many teachers, colleagues, and students, we would still be groping in the dark with this work. The help of doctors Herbert Dandes, Richard Greenbaum, Kate Adler, Nancy Bacher-Watson, Ron Shellow, and others was essential to the validation studies that supported our hypotheses. Doctoral students Janine Osborne, Doug Reichel, and Stephen Gill provided critical background support in the validation of this system.

Finally, we wish to express our deepest gratitude to our wives, Marge Reichenberg and Millie Raphael, for their ever-present willingness to support us throughout the arduous process of developing our ideas into the present book. Their enthusiastic help in all stages of preparation allowed the process to reach its present form.

Advanced Psychodiagnostic Interpretation of the Bender Gestalt Test

Chapter 1

INTRODUCTION

For more than one hundred years, psychologists and others have attempted to measure human personality characteristics. Instruments to measure the unconscious aspects of an individual's personality began to emerge early in this century, largely as a result of the work of those interested in the measurement of human perception.

Historically, however, personality assessment and delineation appeared as early as 460-377 B.C. in the writings of Hippocrates, who suggested that temperament, or personality, was related to the relationships between various bodily fluids. Throughout recorded history, the wish to discern the nature or inner workings of the human spirit was reflected in Western cultural literature. Charles Darwin and Francis Galton propelled scientific exploration into the nature of man and genetics in the mid-nineteenth century. One of the earliest perceptual physiologists, Galton developed primitive techniques to measure human perception as early as 1883. He may have been the first to include a questionnaire in his research. Alfred Binet's work in memory and judgment in 1895 opened the door to the founders of modern personality assessment, Wilhelm Wundt, James Cattell, Charles Spearman, Hermann Rorschach, and others. Emil Kraepelin experimented with word association tests as early as 1892. Rorschach developed the Rorschach Inkblot Test in 1921. Research in human intelligence, perception, memory, and other mental processes mushroomed in the early part of the twentieth century.

The exigencies of World War I brought an impetus for large-scale, cost-effective, time-limited assessment. In the United States, England, Germany and France, recruits and soldiers from culturally diverse backgrounds were assessed for intellectual abilities and personality disturbances. Funding of research and training expanded and the psychometric industry expanded rapidly.

A common theme of contemporary personality researchers was and is the belief that one's productions--verbal, written, or otherwise--reflect one's internal or unconscious perceptions. The externalization, or expression, of internal processes became the focus of clinical practice in psychiatry and psychology. In his 1912 work *Totem and Taboo*, Freud defined the concept of projection for the first time as a method of shaping one's external self.

The projection of inner perception to the outside world is a primitive mechanism, which, for instance, also influences our sense perceptions, so that it normally has the greatest share in shaping our outer world. Under conditions that have not yet been sufficiently determined, even inner perceptions of ideational and emotional processes are projected outwardly, like sense perceptions, and are used to shape the outer world. (pp. 107-8)

L. K. Frank (1939), one of the first post-World War I psychologists interested in the area of projective measures, suggested that individuals handle their inner, "private worlds" through projection in unstructured situations, which could be measured by projective tests. S. J. Beck (1937), who introduced one of the earliest scoring systems for the Rorschach Inkblot projective test, stressed gathering information from tests and not from other sources. Beck, like Frank and others, believed that definitive personality information was outside the person's awareness, and that self-report techniques were thus of limited value.

Another contemporary explanation of the mechanism of projection was offered by David Rapaport et al. in their widely read and still highly respected text *Diagnostic Psychological Testing* (1945). Rapaport's metaphorical explanation was as follows:

The concept of projection as used in projective procedures is one formed on the patterns of projector and screen. In this sense, a projection has occurred when the psychological structure of the subject becomes palpable in his actions, choices, products and creations. Therefore, when a procedure is so designed as to enable the subject to demonstrate his psychological structure unstilted by conventional modes, it is projective. The subject matter used in the procedure serves as a lens of a projector, and the recorded material of elicited behavior is the screen with the picture projected on it. (p. 225)

Interestingly, some of the most significant projective procedures utilized to assess personality traits were in fact created for other pursuits. One of the best examples of this is the Bender Gestalt Test, one of the most widely utilized psychological tests. In 1923 Max Wertheimer, a perceptual psychologist, developed a series of geometric designs to measure human perception. Likewise, psychoanalyst, Paul Schilder (1934) believed that visual-motor perception *includes* the personality operating in a specific task, not exclusively the mechanical act of perceiving. Schilder not only pursued this belief himself, but encouraged his wife, Lauretta Bender, and other researchers to further explore this relationship. Bender, later known for her 1938 publication, *A Visual Motor Test and Its Clinical Use*, used four of Wertheimer's original designs and slightly modified five others in developing the Bender Gestalt Test as a means of "exploring deviations in the maturational process in perceptual motor functions associated with certain pathologic conditions, among which were mental retardation, schizophrenia, organic brain damage, aphasia, manic-depressive psychosis, and certain toxic conditions" (Tolor & Schulberg, 1963).

Bender's work was catapulted into prominence when World War II provided an urgent need for personality tests to diagnose huge numbers of American soldiers who were culturally and geographically dissimilar, more than occasionally illiterate, and often suffering from one of many psychiatric disorders or some degree of organic brain syndrome. Since the Bender Gestalt Test (BGT) could be administered to large groups of soldiers in five to ten minutes, it became one of the most popular tests of that era and has remained one of the five most popular and frequently used tests to assess personality and identify neurologic abnormalities (Cohen et al., 1988; Schulberg & Tolor, 1961; Craig, 1979; Lacks, 1984).

Max Hutt, Lauretta Bender's colleague and co-researcher, was directly involved in the administration of the army testing service during World War II. He published a guide for the interpretation and administration of the Bender in 1945. Since then, Hutt has published over twenty-five books and articles in this area, at least fourteen of which are specifically about the Bender. Presently, for anyone interested in using the Bender as a psychodynamic or projective test, Hutt's work is a leading source. Dissatisfied with Bender's ambivalence toward the use of the test for personality assessment, Hutt and Briskin developed an adaptation of the Bender, the Hutt Adaptation of the Bender Gestalt Test (HABGT), in 1960. They reported using a set of stimulus shapes that they felt were more faithful to Wertheimer's original designs. Analysis and comparison of all three design sets--by Wertheimer, Bender, and Hutt and Briskin--reveals that there are minimal differences between the Bender test and the Hutt adaptation, and the two can be used interchangeably.

Credit for the first published psychodynamic scoring system goes to G. R. Pascal and B. J. Suttell, who published a lengthy and widely used scoring system in 1951. Hutt and Briskin's original system was published in 1960, and its fourth edition was published shortly before Hutt's death in 1985. In 1964, J. D. Hain published an article describing another scoring system but never published the actual system. In 1976, S. J. Paulker published a one-page scoring manual about his own system, but it omitted illustrations of the scoring samples. Psychologist Elizabeth Koppitz (1963, 1975) further developed a personality scoring system for the Bender, listing twelve "emotional indicators" in the scoring of protocols for children (ages 5-11). Patricia Lacks published an adaptation of the Hutt-Briskin method in 1984. However, her system focused on organic rather than psychodynamic utilization of the test. This expansion from personality assessment to neurologic screening is, we believe, a reflection of the versatility of the measure itself.

American academicians, researchers, and clinicians, affected by the surge in cost containment measures of managed health care and the sharply reduced funding in outpatient and inpatient mental health services, are presently seeking expeditious, inexpensive solutions for complex, often chronic problems. The BGT offers quick, relatively culture-free, non-verbal personality and neurologic information that is ideal for group administration, as seen by its widespread clinical use since World War II. Its popularity with American clinicians and academicians has not declined, nor has the popularity of other projective tests, such as the Rorschach, the Thematic Apperception Test, and various drawing tests (Piotrowski, 1985). In a summary of 114 psychology departments in public adult psychiatric hospitals, Paul L. Craig (1979) found that the BGT was the most frequently cited test, used by fourteen hundred psychologists in neuropsychological evaluations, with over 74 percent of the hospitals indicating its use. In a ten-year study conducted by Barry Ritzler and Barbara Alter (1986), it was found that 88 percent of all APA-approved graduate clinical psychology programs in the United States and Canada place major emphasis on the Rorschach in at least one assessment course, as compared to 86 percent in 1974, suggesting an increase in projective assessment training of psychologists over the decade.

Despite widespread clinical usage, projective assessment has met strong competition from the less accurate but inexpensively implemented self-report measures. The ambivalence to projective testing is, we believe, attributable to three professional issues. First, despite strong cultural support, psychometrically oriented personality theorists, "wedded to their questionnaires disregard the general uselessness of self-report instruments, choosing instead to ignore the unconscious and rely on what their subjects tell them," yielding inaccurate and often disastrous information (McClelland, 1981). Also, computerization has led to a proliferation of actuarially developed inventories and questionnaires, which rely almost exclusively on self-report procedures. Current teachings in psychology are ambivalent about the worth of self-report personality measures.

Personality tests that employ self-report methodologies have both advantages and disadvantages. On the one hand, the person answering the question is - assuming sound judgement and insight - among the people best qualified to provide the most accurate answers. On the other hand, the person may possess neither good judgement nor good insight. And regardless of judgement or insight, respondents might be unwilling to reveal anything that could place them in a negative light. *A need existed for personality tests that did not rely heavily on a respondent's own self-report.* (Cohen et al., 1988, pp. 34-35, emphasis added)

Second, while statistical findings are important, clinicians dealing with an individual are attuned to subjectively analyzed material that provides insight into unconsciously constructed personality traits and functioning. For example, knowing that 82 percent of a group have a higher or lower potential for self-harm does not carry much meaning when addressing the potential reality for self-harm of a given person. One of the unfortunate results of reliance on objective tests is clearly explained by Chris Piotrowsky, Dave Sherry, and John Keller (1985):

Much of the projective test misuse has been due to inadequate basic training in the universities. People who do not really know testing, nor who have had extensive clinical experience are often assigned to teach these courses. They cannot extract the rich clinical information contained in a test battery, cannot do blind analyses, and, as a result, cannot teach or lead students adequately in this area. Consequently, the validity of these tests has been underestimated, since they are often used improperly or superficially without the extensive and intensive training and experience needed for their appropriate application. (pp. 115-19)

Third, some underutilization of projective testing is also attributable to negative research methodology, or critical studies that have used inappropriate validation procedures. Often, empirical rather than conceptual validation procedures have been used to evaluate the worth of projective tests. The most notable, of course, is the Rorschach inkblots. Empirical research on the Rorschach, including but not limited to Samuel Haramis and Edwin Wagner (1980), and A. R. Jensen (1965), compares two or more treatment samples across random Rorschach measures to assess which occur more frequently in one sample versus another. Conceptual studies, including but not limited to Zygmunt Piotrowski (1965), Irving Weiner (1977), Richard Dana (1978), and L. Atkinson et al. (1986), in contrast with empirical studies, try to offer some explanation as to why the measures in question are relevant to the differentiation attempted.

Atkinson et al. investigated forty-six Rorschach validation studies, collected from every fifth year of the psychological abstracts, from 1930 to 1980. They found that inadequate research methodology, rather than the Rorschach itself, was partially responsible for criticism of the test. They concluded that "the future lies in the direction of better conceptualized research" (Atkinson et al, 1986, p. 362).

While these studies focused on the Rorschach, we believe that the results are generalizable to the BGT and other projective tests. Despite previously negative research, Chris Piotrowski, Dave Sherry and John Keller (1985) surveyed the membership of the Society for Personality Assessment and found that the Rorschach was the most frequently employed projective measure.

Our view, shared by many others, is that if projective tests are used cautiously and with ample training, clinicians and researchers can use them to extract accurate psychodiagnostic impressions that cannot be obtained without otherwise spending months in therapeutic investigative work. Additionally, we believe that no single test, without exception, is adequate to accurately assess the complexity of dynamic forces within an individual.

As an initial measure in a battery of tests, the BGT provides an integral screening or checklist against which the ensuing psychological tests can confirm or rule out its various hypotheses. Like a barometer, the responses to the Bender designs forecast areas of turbulence or disturbance which, once noted and understood, aid the clinician in increasing diagnostic accuracy. Clinicians often lean heavily on one measure, usually the Rorschach Inkblots or the

Minnesota Multiphasic Personality Inventory - Revised (MMPI-R), rather than using a wide group of personality measures. This is largely attributable to expedience, poor training or cost containment. Interviews cannot provide the accuracy of powerful projective tests, as seen in research on the validity of interviews (Tenopyr, 1981; Ulrich & Trumbo, 1965). We cannot emphasize strongly enough that the use of a psychological battery is critical when one is engaged in assessing a personality in any setting.

The purpose of this book is to offer a new means of extending and increasing the dynamic personality assessment usage of the Bender Gestalt or the HABGT.

The well-known works of Bender (1938), Koppitz (1963; 1975), Lacks (1984), and Hutt (1969) have formulated the basis upon which our approach can be used to increase the depth and meaningfulness of interpretations from BGT responses. The BGT, when interpreted thusly, quickly provides unique idiosyncratic information vital to accurate personality assessment and, if necessary, to meaningful therapy. Based on the current emphasis on short-term treatment and the pressure to understand a patient's dynamics expeditiously, our system provides the greater likelihood of positive therapeutic outcome. In essence, if you understand the unconscious conflicts of a patient (child or adult), you are less likely to be misled by pseudosymptomatology stressed by conscious content. The Bender Gestalt Test's previous scoring systems have somewhat underutilized its potential as a projective personality test, and the present work helps deepen one's capability of assessing the human psyche. Our system was developed over thirty years of clinical experience, with over twenty thousand subjects of diverse ethnic and educational representation, from ages 6 to 92.

The Bender Gestalt and the HABGT, when interpreted and scored as described in the following chapters, will serve as an accurate infrastructure for the remainder of the psychological evaluation.

Chapter 2

ADMINISTRATION

In the standard or traditional psychological test battery, the usual approach is to begin by having the individual being evaluated fill out a biographical information or intake form. Our administration of the Bender Gestalt Test or the Hutt Adaptation, immediately following the completion of the intake form, is similar to the instructions given by Bender in her monograph (1938), with minimal changes. The reason for the changes will be given in the following directions.

Several sheets of paper are placed vertically before the individual being evaluated. Several sharpened pencils with erasers are provided. All nine Bender or Hutt cards are placed above and parallel to the paper, facing the patient. The nine cards are placed face up in ascending order with Card A on top. The instructions are given to simply, "Copy what you see onto the paper in front of you as carefully as possible, and while you have plenty of paper, do not put one design to a page." The reasons for asking for more than one design per page will be discussed shortly.

While it may seem obvious, pens should not be allowed, since the distortions in line quality are not easily noticed and erasures are impossible. Pencil is also much more productive in terms of line thickness and shading possibilities, not only in the Bender but in all written responses to the projective tests (i.e., the House-Tree-Person and the Sentence Completion Tests) and the information sheet, which may vary from examiner to examiner but usually provides clinically important information. Tempo and sequence is significant in dealing with any of the nine Bender designs, as well as many other psychological tests. How quickly or slowly one responds to a test stimuli is often a significant projection of personality traits. In terms of interrelations, differences in line quality among the various figures will also be used in interpretation.

As the copy is made, the examiner makes sure that the finished design card is turned over and placed to the side before the individual starts on the next design. How the discarded designs are handled can be diagnostic and should be noted. A classic example of this as significant was the handling of Card 3 (the male sexual and aggression card) by an 8-year-old female who, it was later discovered, had a sexual abuse history that was both physically and legally documented. Upon completion of each design, this child would place the card to her left on the desk. However, after completing Card 3, she placed the card inside the top desk drawer. After she had completed the ninth and final card, the examiner showed her the eight remaining cards and asked her what had happened to the missing card. She replied, "I don't know," looked around and under the desk, opened the top drawer again, looked inside, and closed the drawer without "seeing" the card therein. This behavior was a clinical example of dissociation resulting from earlier sexual trauma.

The paper used for reproduction of the designs may be turned by the subject, but turning of the Bender cards is to be discouraged. Many subjects like to turn the cards however, and this is often a reflection of manipulative personality traits. For consistency, the cards should not be turned, and attempts to turn them should be noted and then discouraged.

The authors agree with Bender's statements, given in her directions, that this is a clinical test and should not be rigidly formulated. However, our basis for disallowing the turning of the cards stems from our emphasis on interpretation of the relationships among the figures; we can interpret these relationships more definitively if the cards are not turned.

Care should be taken, as with all projective measures, that "advice" or more elaborate directions not be given, particularly when the subject or patient appears to be dependent or looking for outside help. Responses to questions should be as open-ended as possible. The responses should be succinct, but at no time should the subject be told how to duplicate the designs. At most, a statement that the designs vary in difficulty might be offered to a particularly anxious individual.

With regard to test anxiety, because it is seemingly simple and nonthreatening, the use of the Bender as the first "test" usually results in an obvious reduction in test anxiety, and this is extremely helpful in obtaining certain projective responses, not only to the Bender but also to more anxiety-producing projective measures. Based on past experience, starting with projective drawings, for example, creates far greater anxiety than does starting with the Bender designs. The Bender helps to place the individual at ease and provides a quicker means of establishing some rapport.

The above instructions are similar to those suggested by Bender in her monograph *A Visual Motor Test and Its Clinical Use* (1938) and by Hutt in his book, *The Hutt Adaptation of the Bender Gestalt Test* (1960). The importance of reducing test anxiety cannot be overstated.

It is also of major importance that the duplication of designs be *observed by the examiner*; since important clinical information can be lost if the drawing of the designs is not observed and the handling (e.g., in terms of negativism) is ignored. For example, it is of clinical significance if Card 6 is duplicated from the right-hand edge of the page to the left, rather than the more typical left to right.

The possibility of deviations due to left-handedness or right-handedness has been considered in the past, and no significant findings regarding left- or right-handed differences in the duplication of the designs was found. That is, both left- and right-handed people generally duplicate the designs from left to right. Nevertheless, the clinician must be aware of possible cultural differences; for instance, Semitic individuals expressing their anger and dissatisfaction may deliberately do all the designs from right to left. A major example of this was the case of an imprisoned terrorist assassin, who emphasized his Semitic heritage as an excuse for the severe acting-out behavior in which he had been engaged.

It is assumed that clinicians will be using the patient's comments or questions concerning the Bender as projective material, and it is difficult to give instructions to cover every variation of response given by the client. One must be cognizant of what is meant by the questions asked and what is meant by the behavior observed. It is the clinician's responsibility to reduce test anxiety. For graduate students and beginning professionals, the adage that "less is more" should be followed, both in obtaining the Bender and in dealing any with other projective measure. For example, Pascal and Suttell (1951) state in their instructions that there are nine designs; others do not give a number. We usually do not give the patient the number of designs, but we do insist that one design per page is not acceptable.

The most frequently asked question by patients concerns whether "counting the dots" is permissible (Cards 1, 2, 3, 5). The least amount of structure given by the clinician is basically the most valuable, and the reproduction of the designs, including the number of dots, is open to interpretation. We suggest that the individual asking this particular question simply be told "Duplicate them or copy them as you see them." If the dots are not counted, the resulting reproductions are open to interpretation in terms of clinical meaning (e.g., test anxiety, uncritical behavior, and/or severe impulsivity).

There is no time limit for administration of the Bender, but unusually slow or quick responses can be diagnostic. There are differences in opinion among experts concerning the amount of time that should be allotted to administration, but our experience suggests that it is more meaningful to interpret the way the time was spent than to limit the time given. For example, designs that are completed with excess speed and a concomitant lack of self-criticalness certainly can be interpreted in terms of the indicated dynamics. On the other hand, obsessive-compulsive or anxiety-ridden individuals trying ever so carefully to reproduce perfect designs are also giving valuable information in terms of their dynamics. The time should not be limited unless, in the clinician's opinion, the amount of time being spent reflects more of a significant resistance aspect than a considered effort.

In our system of interpretation, the individual is not encouraged to start at the upper left-hand corner of the page with the initial figure, as suggested by Bender. If the first figure is placed in the center of the page and enlarged however, the individual can be told, "That was my mistake; I don't want one design per page. Would you put more than one design on a sheet of paper?" If the subject then asks, "How many sheets of paper?", the response should be, "You can use as many as you like, as long as you don't place one design per page." Having been told that there is plenty of paper, but that the examiner does not want one design to a single page, the individual is then free to use one or more sheets for the design.

Similarly, according to Bender's manual (1938), erasures "may be permitted but not encouraged." In our system, the erasures contribute a great deal in terms of where and when they occur, and while they are not specifically encouraged, the erasures should not be discouraged. Generally, erasures reflect self-criticalness and/or anxiety.

Environmental factors, of course, are of major importance. It is always hoped that the reproductions will be obtained in a quiet, well-lit, stimulus-free situation, but in practice this is not always true. For example, the individual undergoing the evaluation may be in a school setting, a hospital setting, a personnel selection setting or a jail setting. While the conditions may not be pristine, the handling of the projective measures should still be possible if the clinician makes allowances for less than perfect testing settings. The validity of the interpretations will not ordinarily depend on environmental factors. External distortions should be handled in terms of the clinician's own experience in dealing with projective measures. The functioning clinician must often work in less than ideal situations, and it is essential to be able to do so.

It is also important to keep in mind that the Bender represents one projective test in a battery of projective tests. Used dynamically, it can serve as a source of greater understanding in dealing with the entire protocol regarding the dynamics of the individual being evaluated.

Chapter 3

CARD A

We have designated Card A as the parental figure card. This, of course, does not imply restriction to biological parents. Rather, psychological parenthood related to gender is delineated on this design. In actuality this could be a grandparent, parent, or parental older sibling, depending on the specifics. For example, when either or both biologic parents are unavailable, a growing number of individuals are reared, at least in their formative years, by grandparents or older siblings. The female/maternal portion of the figure is the circle figure; the male/paternal portion of the symbol is the figure that is square. If one figure is drawn higher than the other, even if that difference is minuscule, the interpretation can be made that the higher figure represents the dominant parental figure. If the square penetrates the circle, the obvious interpretation should be made in terms of a physically aggressive father figure, and conversely, an aggressive mother figure is suggested if the circle overlaps the square. By observing the actual drawing of the figure, the examiner will be able to discern which figure intersects or overlaps. If there is a separation of the two figures, the resulting interpretation would be in terms of separated, underinvolved parental figures, at least. Very often, in reproductions by children of divorced or divorcing parents, the separation of these figures is gross and obvious.

As stated in the chapter on administration, if the individual starts by copying Design A in the center of the page, the request by the examiner concerning more than one figure on a page should be made. If the individual continues by placing the subsequent designs below the initial figure, the importance of the parental figures in the ongoing dynamics should be upgraded. If, however, subsequent designs are placed around, that is, above and to the sides of Figure A, overwhelming turmoil involving parental figures is suggested and can be expected to be confirmed in the other projective measures used in this test battery. Of course, the older the subject, the greater the likelihood of severe psychopathology and gross immaturity.

A distortion of the circle in terms of an incomplete circle is considered to reflect deficient nurture by the mother figure; an incomplete diamond is considered to reflect deficient nurture by the father figure.

If the individual puts Design A in the center of the page and the figures are very large, it is most effective in terms of assessing dynamics to start over, telling the patient, "I didn't make myself clear enough; would you start again and not put one design on a page?" On such occasions, if the subject then attempts to complete all nine designs in the upper portion of a page, this could be interpreted as anger at feeling criticized, or more accurately, as an artificial attempt by the patient to demonstrate more impulse control than is typically available to the individual. This occurs most often in criminal court evaluations, where the impulsivity and acting-out pressures are masked by the individual in order to give a more positive picture of himself or herself. When this artificial constriction occurs, it usually involves individuals with defective egos who have trouble maintaining control over their impulses (e.g., acting-out psychopaths and sociopaths).

It must be remembered that any aspect of the reproduction can provide information regarding personality structure. For example, whether the line quality is light or heavy and whether all lines are the same consistency or there is variability should provide some information regarding the subject's feelings or attitudes toward either or both parents. By parents, as mentioned earlier, these do not have to be biological parents, but may be parental figures.

The following case illustrations have been drawn from the authors' clinical research and have been validated, both by referring professionals and by other personality measures in the battery. Reproductions of the drawings discussed in the case analyses can be found at the end of each chapter. Wherever possible, the drawings have been positioned to reflect the subjects' placement of them on an 8 1/2 x 11 sheet of paper and, unless otherwise noted, are reproduced at full size. Each drawing is identified by the sex and age (years followed by months) of the individual.

The first example of a significant Card A distortion is of a 13-year, 5-month-old female (see Plate 3.1). The diamond dominates both figures and penetrates into the female circle symbol. In addition, the circle is not complete. The finishing lines cross, are darker, and in keeping with previous statements, suggest a feeling of anger due to nurture deprivation in this girl. The likelihood of an aggressive father should be considered and, depending on further projective measures or interview data, should be confirmed or denied. The failure to complete the diamond while penetrating the circle is a strong indication of aggression in the father figure. Of further significance regarding the demonstration figure is the failure of the bottom lines of the father figure to intersect properly which would suggest that the male parental figure was seen not only as aggressive, but also as nonnurturing.

This girl had been molested, and the turmoil involving the parental figures was confirmed both in terms of her history when hospitalized and in terms of other projective measures.

The second example was done by a 38-year-old woman involved in a child custody dispute (Plate 3.2). The parental figure designs of Card A show an overidentification of this individual with the mother figure, in that the circle is larger and far more dominant than the diamond. Other responses in the protocol were consistent with this finding, as was the clinical record. For example, she stated in her Sentence Completion Form that "A MOTHER CANNOT neglect her child"--as she herself was incapable of doing. The inconsistent line quality would reflect her ambivalence regarding the attachment to the mother figure, and the extremely narrow diamond would reflect her tendency to feel that the father figure was nonnurturing. In addition, the incomplete diamond, as seen in the opening of the upper angle, would be interpreted as an aggressive father figure. The overwhelming need to be "feminine" resulted in her being vulnerable to male dominance and subsequently depressed, as noted in the other projective measures. This also appeared in terms of fluctuating control, as noted in Card 1 of her Bender and in her involvement with drug usage as a means of dealing with constant dissatisfaction with self.

The third example was done by a 14-year, 7-month-old boy (Plate 3.3). It reflects a nurture-deficient mother symbol, with the end lines not meeting, and more importantly, the presence of an aggressive and possibly abusive father figure, by the penetration of the diamond into the circle. At the time of the evaluation, this child had regressed to psychotic functioning and had been referred by a child analyst for a psychological workup. The darker line quality and crisscrossed corners of the diamond also suggest that females were demeaned by the father, resulting in this boy's severely impaired self-concept and identification with an aggressive and abusive father. Confirmation of the above interpretations was found in the other personality measures and in the follow-up with the referring psychiatrist.

The fourth example of Card A, that of a 14-year-old male, shows the parental figures significantly separated, reflecting the loss or absence of a parental figure, in this case the father (Plate 3.4). Distortions in terms of lack of affective interaction with parental figures is often seen when the figures are not touching. The separation of these figures often suggests that there is a lack of intimacy with parents, and that the parents are not communicating effectively. In addition, the separation often permits the child to come between the parents and play both ends against the middle in terms of his or her own overt behavior. This boy had serious behavior problems and his parents were divorced. His father had not seen him in two years.

Plate 3.1
Card A by a 13.5-year-old Female

Plate 3.3
Card A by a 14.7-year-old Male

Plate 3.4
Card A by a 14-year-old Male

REVIEW QUESTIONS

1. Card A could represent

   a. biological parental figures.
   b. psychological parental figures.
   c. parentified older siblings or grandparents.
   d. all of the above.

2. The line quality of the figures reflects

   a. organicity.
   b. psychosis.
   c. the subject's affect.
   d. parental inconsistency.

3. If the figures do not touch,

   a. the patient is schizophrenic.
   b. the patient is organically impaired.
   c. the patient has gender identity problems.
   d. the patient's parents were not close.

4. If the circle is higher on the page than is the diamond,

   a. the patient is manic-depressive.
   b. the patient is a multiple personality.
   c. the patient's father is not the psychological parent.
   d. none of the above.

Chapter 4

CARD 1

The next card, Card 1, reflects the individual's ability to control impulses. The line of dots, from left to right, represents one's life span and, deviations in the reproduction of this design reflect impulse control deficits from infancy to the present age. If the subject draws fewer dots than the number of dots on the card, that person's impulse controls are seen as tenuous. If there are more than the correct number of dots, a preoccupation with control is likely, and if there is an extreme extension of the line of dots across the page, the preoccupation may have reached psychotic proportions.

In addition, the slope of the line is significant. If the slant is predominately downward (from left to right), it is likely that further psychological personality test material will also suggest ongoing depression. Conversely, if the slope of the line is upward, from left to right, the acting-out potential increases in keeping with the angle of ascension. The greater the ascension, the greater the emphasis on poor impulse control and acting-out. If there is noticeable variability in terms of a downward and upward handling of the line (i.e., a wavy line), fluctuation would be expected in the individual's ability to deal with impulses.

Regression from dots to circles, the most common form of distortion, is another significant factor. It reflects regression in affective functioning, a lower level of emotional maturation and a higher probability of disturbed functioning in the area symbolically represented by the card. In addition, a change from dots to slash marks on Card 1 suggests that the individual is apt to engage in openly aggressive and hostile acting-out behavior.

The area or location of distortions on this figure gives some indication of the primitiveness of the loss of control. If the expansiveness in terms of dots to circles occurs near the left end of the line of dots, the frustration tolerance of the individual is extremely low, and similarly, the ability to control impulses (e.g., obey rules) is poor. The handling of this figure is of particular significance when related to other personality measures such as the Rorschach Inkblots, by which impulse control is evaluated.

If the drawing of the dots ends up against either side edge of the page, the interpretation would be in terms of the individual needing or seeking environmental limits for impulsivity. He or she would be prone to rule breaking, illegal behavior, poor reliability, and dishonesty. Also, variability in the dot structure is extremely important, especially in relation to other personality measures in the evaluation dealing with potential danger of acting out against self or others. The earlier the deviations from the model occur in the line of dots (from left to right), the more chronic and pronounced the acting-out disturbance. This would be reflected in terms of the degree of severity in the impaired superego. Often these individuals are extremely manipulative, oppositional, and lacking in insight or self-awareness.

When dots are duplicated in pairs by the individual, obsessive-compulsive pressures and, more likely, paranoid features are to be expected in the protocol. The more pronounced the separation of pairs, the more pronounced the paranoid pressures. These individuals are mistrustful, sensitive to inferred or real derision, and are generally difficult in endeavors requiring team effort.

When there are marked gaps or spaces between the dots, it raises the possibility of erratic control of impulses, particularly if the shading also fluctuates from dark to light or vice-versa. Regression from dots to open circles deals both with excessive dependency needs and the presence of intense anger. The variation of dots to circles in some of the dotted figures and not in others would be interpreted in terms of where the regression occurred and on what figure. If the individual uses circles instead of dots on any design, the regression would be tied to the dynamics of that particular design. That is, circles for dots in reproducing Card 1 suggest regression and reduced effective control over one's impulses. The clinician would have to evaluate where circle-to-dot behavior occurs on the other dotted figures, Card 3 and Card 5. If circles are used for dots on all or most of the dotted figures, the intensity of regression is high and the possibility of psychotic functioning is very likely.

If the regression from dots to circles occurs to selected figures involving dots, the interpretation would be enhanced in significance in terms of which figure shows the regression. The following case illustrations will amplify the reader's understanding of the preceding interpretations.

The first example is from an 11-year-old boy from an upper-middle-class family (Plate 4.1). His reluctance to complete the design, combined with the spacing that begins to occur, suggests that he is out of control as far as the environment is concerned and that he is in need of psychotherapeutic intervention. The incomplete design is consistent with the regression from dots to circles on the right-hand side, suggesting that his reaction to his parents' recent divorce had overwhelmed his defenses in terms of ongoing anger and greatly increased his impulsivity.

Confirmation of the above was obtained clinically and from other psychological measures, and the child was placed in therapy.

The second example is from a 16-year, 10-month-old girl seen in an adolescent psychiatric unit, hospitalized due to depression and behavioral turmoil (Plate 4.2). The downward slope of the line is in keeping with overt and covert indications of depression, and in addition, the design was carefully numbered. Numbering the designs reflects a conscious effort to demonstrate better controls than are actually available. Also of significance in her handling of Card 1 was the increasing thickness of the dot quality in the middle of the line and subsequent retreat to less definite dots toward the end. As stated previously, the handling of these dots deals with impulse control, and this subject evidenced, clinically, a significant and often self-derogatory handling of impulsive demands. For example, there was an attempt at self-harm, which while superficially could be seen as manipulative, actually represented a dangerous underlying depression.

The third example is the reproduction of Card 1 by a 48-year-old male (Plate 4.3). The extension of the dots from one side of the page to the next reflected the ideational turmoil and preoccupation that was interfering with his overall functioning. Not only was he unable to deal with the ongoing disturbed ideation, but the controls indicated in his reproduction suggested that there was significant variability in his handling of everyday demands. In keeping with this would be his beginning with the dots close together and, as he proceeded across the page, his regression of dots almost into circles, which become more widely separated. The significant interpretation of this design was in terms of the availability of meaningful controls for this seriously disturbed individual. Confirmation of his regression and inability to function effectively appeared in the other measures and also was confirmed by the clinical findings. The downward slope in the center of the line and the overwhelming depression that caused him to seek help were immediately reconfirmed in his bare and barren tree drawing for the House-Tree-Person Drawing Test. He used cocaine on a daily basis and his wife initiated divorce proceedings just prior to his evaluation.

The fourth example (Plate 4.4) is from the 14-year, 7-month-old boy mentioned in Chapter 3 (Plate 3.3). His handling of Card 1 will be discussed here and in Chapter 5 in relation to the interaction of this reproduction with that of Card 2. Card 1 reflects the regression, as indicated in the circles instead of dots. Effective control over impulses would be correspondingly diminished for this child. In addition, Card 1 is seen in terms of his significant variability in the formation of dots; as previously stated, the corresponding interpretations regarding dependency, exaggeration, and anger would hold true for his handling of this design. The child was having extreme difficulty in functioning with even reasonable effectiveness, and this was becoming increasingly evident to the parental figures from his overt behavior, resulting in his parents seeking help. The collision of the control line of Card 1 with Card 2 would emphasize the serious affective disturbances and difficulty in maintaining impulse control in this child. Greater clarification of his conscious affect will be delineated in Chapter 5.

Plate 4.1
Card 1 by an 11-year-old Male

Plate 4.2
Card 1 by a 16.10-year-old Female

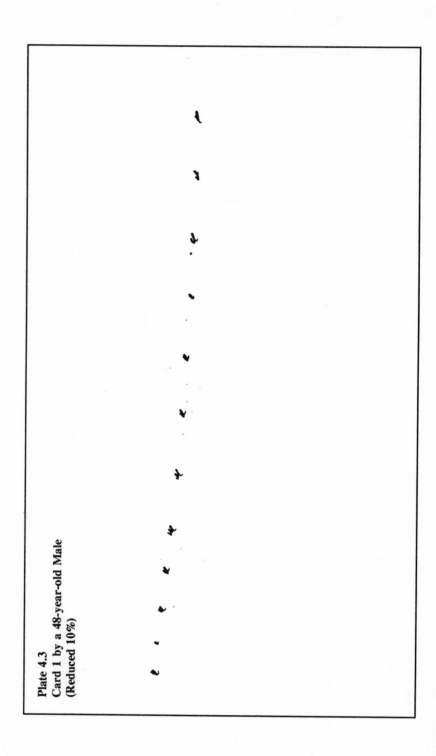

Plate 4.3
Card 1 by a 48-year-old Male
(Reduced 10%)

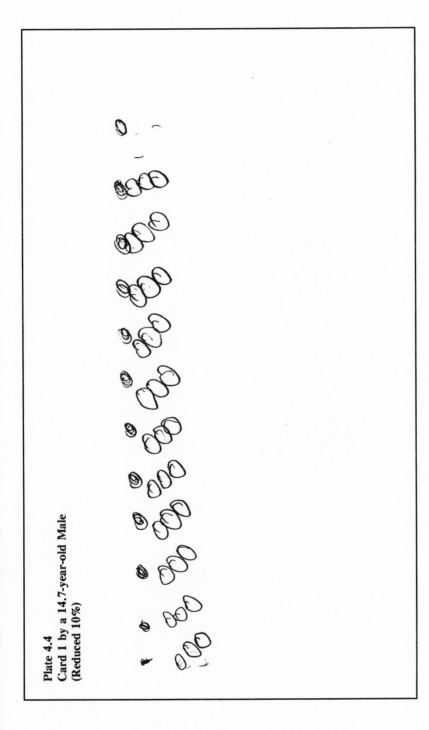

Plate 4.4
Card 1 by a 14.7-year-old Male
(Reduced 10%)

25

REVIEW QUESTIONS

1. If there are more than twelve dots,

    a. the patient is depressed.
    b. the patient is organically impaired.
    c. the patient's impulse controls are tenuous.
    d. the patient's preoccupation with control is impairing functioning.

2. If the line is made of pairs of dots,

    a. the patient has visual myopia.
    b. the patient is compulsive.
    c. the patient may reflect paranoia.
    d. none of the above.

3. If there are uneven gaps or spaces between the dots,

    a. the patient uses intellectualization.
    b. the patient is organically impaired.
    c. the patient is depressed.
    d. none of the above.

4. If the dots anywhere in this line are open circles,

    a. extreme anger and dependency is likely.
    b. schizophrenia is likely.
    c. the patient needs and seeks environmental restrictions.
    d. none of the above.

Chapter 5

CARD 2

Card 2 is interpreted in terms of conscious affect, conscious dissatisfaction, and conscious dysphoria. The line of dots descending or ascending can be interpreted as with Card 1; that is, the affect is dealt with at conscious levels, and the greater the deviation from the model, the more pronounced the disturbance. The subjects usually have greater difficulty in maintaining the direction of the circles on Design 2, and they will often express exasperation at not being able to get the angle right. The more pronounced the disturbance, the greater the tendency to carry the ascending slope of the design through Design 1.

If the lines of three circles lose their angulation, intense conscious depression should be present, and the greater the loss of angulation, the more severe is that depression. Also, the earlier in the design (from left to right) the loss of angulation occurs, the greater the chronicity of the affective disorder.

If Design 2 collides with Design 1, it is likely that the subject has extreme difficulty in maintaining effective controls over his or her impulses. Very often, individuals will attempt to erase their reproduction of this design as it begins to approach or collide with Design 1. The effectiveness of correction following erasure offers the possibility for interpreting the ability of these individuals to "correct" their behavior.

Excessive spaces between the various lines of circles (i.e., a significant separation between one row of three circles and another) suggest dissociation and can be confirmed in other measures of dissociative tendencies (i.e., the Rorschach Inkblots, the MMPI-2). If the circles butt up against the side of the page or the top of the page, the individual is seeking environmental limits for his or her acting-out anti-social behavior.

If any of the circles are closed and colored in, the anger reflected is more pronounced. Of course, the greater the number of closed and colored in circles, the greater the possibility of aggressive, overt psychopathic acting-out. If, as occasionally happens, the vertical line of three circles is increased to four or more, the presence of acute schizophrenic processes may be suggested.

The first example (Plate 5.1) is that of the 14-year, 7-month-old boy who was the last example in Chapter 4 (Plate 4.4). It suggests the difficulty he was having in dealing with his affective pressures, and the limited controls mentioned in the previous chapter are reflected in the collision between Design 2 and Design 1. In addition, the separation of the three circles disappears after the second row, and the circles increase in size after the sixth row, suggesting the conscious affective turmoil and disturbance in this extremely angry and overly dependent boy. This appeared repeatedly in the overall protocol, and again, confirmation from the clinical picture was obtained.

The second example (Plate 5.2) is by the 48-year-old male whose handling of Card 1 was discussed in Chapter 4 (Plate 4.3). The perseveration shown in Card 1 reflects a reliance on the environment to limit his acting-out behavior and appears again in his handling of Card 2. In addition, there is a significant deangulation of the first four vertical rows of circles, suggesting ongoing depression that he is attempting to deny, via the fifth through eleventh rows, where the expected angulation of vertical rows appears. There is a significant gap or separation between the fifth and sixth rows and also between the sixth and seventh rows that suggests that his denial and possible dissociative episodes are a means of handling his ideational turmoil and the accompanying depression.

The third example is that of a 26-year-old female psychologist who was referred for evaluation (Plate 5.3). She was unable to deal with the angulation aspect of Card 2, and the design is seen as ascending almost vertically. The disparity involved in her almost total loss of control in duplicating Card 2, as compared with all of her other designs, suggested that conscious dissatisfactions had increased to the extent that she was actively seeking professional help for the ongoing ideational turmoil and accompanying depression. Verification of the interpretation was obtained through the overall clinical picture and her subsequent involvement in therapy.

The fourth example is the reproduction of Card 2 by a 13-year, 5-month-old boy (Plate 5.4). His conscious self-dissatisfaction was evident in that he immediately crossed out his first effort and began again. Of additional significance was the downward curve of the overall design and loss of angulation in the rows of circles as he continued. This was in keeping with his intense ongoing depression and his efforts to constrict and deny these feelings. His attempts, however, proved unsuccessful, and he was hospitalized due to a suicide attempt.

Plate 5.1
Card 2 by a 14.7-year-old Male
(Reduced 10%)

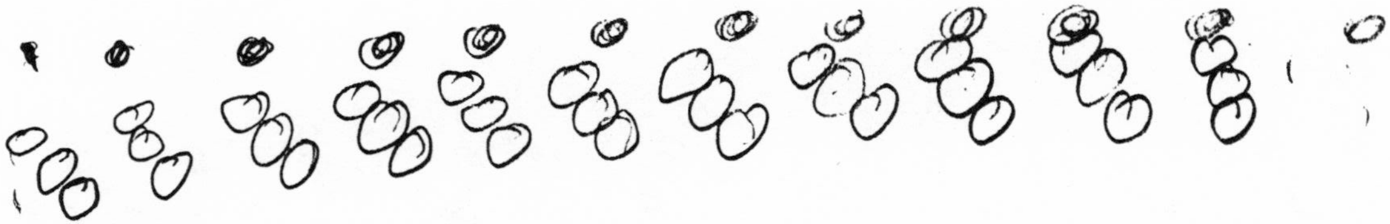

Plate 5.2
Card 2 by a 48-year-old Male
(Reduced 10%)

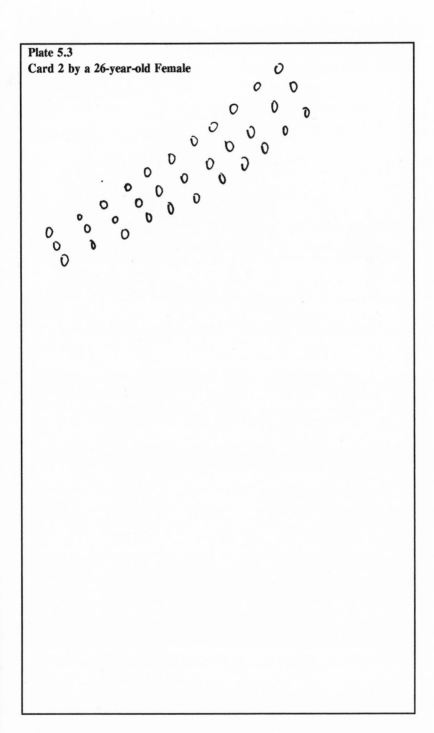

Plate 5.3
Card 2 by a 26-year-old Female

Plate 5.4
Card 2 by a 13.5-year-old Male

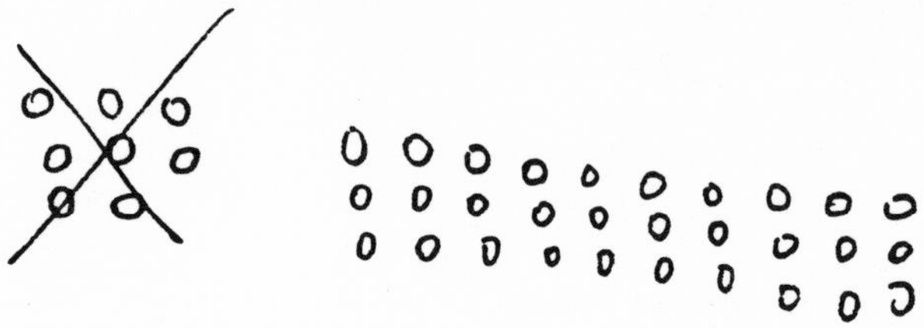

REVIEW QUESTIONS

1. If the lines of dots ascend,

   a. the patient uses projection and repression.
   b. the patient is depressed and lethargic.
   c. the patient is immature and impulsive.
   d. all of the above.

2. If any of the lines has 4 dots, consider

   a. depression.
   b. organicity.
   c. visual deficits.
   d. schizophrenia.

3. The earlier the drawing deviates from the model,

   a. the brighter the patient.
   b. the more the patient is mildly neurotic.
   c. the more pronounced the disturbance.
   d. all of the above.

4. If any circles are closed,

   a. the patient uses repression.
   b. the patient's anger is more pronounced.
   c. the patient's mother was very nurturing.
   d. none of the above.

Chapter 6

CARD 3

This chapter deals with Card 3, the dotted arrow design that reflects one's handling of hostility and sexuality and is referred to as a sexual aggression symbol. Gross sexual turmoil and sado-masochism, as often seen in sexual battery cases, can be partially assessed in interpreting this design. The dotted arrow is a particularly meaningful symbol in the design series, and care should be taken in interpreting the meaning of the reproduction in terms of whether or not the arrow penetrates or comes close to one of the other cards. Since each of the designs represents some aspect of unconscious functioning, the more specific interpretation will depend on which other design the point of the arrow either intersects or comes close to intersecting. This is a particularly useful area for the assessment of sexual acting-out, because the arrow, representing a penis symbol, is useful in assessing libidinal pressures.

Any erasures or diversions from the diagram are suggestive of some confusion between sex and aggression. If the design is drawn, then erased and made smaller by a male patient, he has not adequately separated from mother. What he is saying, basically, is that he "would rather be a child again." The reduction of the drawing really represents intense concerns regarding erectile sufficiency, in that erections symbolize masculine potency. If the design is drawn, then erased and made smaller by a female patient, there may be pathological concerns and fears regarding penetration. It is as if she is saying that potent, sexually aroused males cause her to feel anxious.

The number of dots in each line of the arrow is also significant in that an increase in the number of dots in any line reflects increasing hostility and anger, while a decrease in the number of dots in any line suggests denial and rejection of aggression. If a change in the number of dots occurs behind the longest line (seven dots), the anger is hidden and denied at conscious levels.

If the dots are drawn as open circles, the ideational turmoil and subsequent regression should be considered in the interpretation of this design. Men who draw open circles instead of dots often are expressing concern regarding disturbances in sexual pressures and often are confused and incapable of separating sexual drive from aggressive drives. Although their anger is directed toward the father figure, these men often confuse sex with aggression and may become dangerous to women, children, or other males, in terms of general overt violence or sexual assault. Women who draw open circles often strongly dislike both men and sexual intercourse.

In terms of organicity, while it is clearly beyond the scope of this text to discuss the extensive neuropsychological interpretations of the BGT, a subtle, previously unreported neuropsychological indicator can be found in this design. Specifically, if the horizontal, midline row of dots is not reproduced in a straight line, this may be an indication of neurologic impairment. Of course, this finding should correspond with other more traditional indicators of organicity.

The first example is from a 23-year-old male (Plate 6.1). The conjunction of the dotted arrow design with the mother symbol in Card A is well documented. His reproduction of the mother symbol has inconsistent line quality and exaggerated end points suggesting a nonnurturing figure. The father symbol is seen as aggressive and is penetrating the female figure. In addition, there are openings and projections in the father figure suggesting that the father figure was abusive and nonnurturing. The regression from dots to circles in the arrow figure, as stated above, represents the anger and confusion between sex and aggression, particularly in males. The near collision between the arrow and the mother area of Card A suggests anger towards women that has reach psychotic proportions. The interpretation would involve potentially dangerous acting-out behavior, specifically towards women, in an identification with an aggressive father figure. In actuality, the individual who produced this example was in jail charged with sexual battery, and according to the information obtained, his father was unknown and absent.

The second example was drawn by a 30-year-old female (Plate 6.2). The entire figure of dots was drawn as circles emphasizing her covert rage. The covert expression of her hostility was seen in the constriction of the length of the overall drawing. The absence of erasure suggests a lack of self-criticalness often noted in sociopathic, characterologically disturbed individuals. The interpretations were verified by the facts of the case. She had a history of passive-aggressive antisocial crimes and was in jail charged with arson.

The hostility value of this symbol in terms of interpretation can not be exaggerated, since it's clinical validity has been confirmed for many years. A detailed explanation of the entire Bender of this individual will be discussed in Chapter 12, since the information obtained from the interrelationship of the designs was seen as enormously valuable in understanding the psychotic functioning of this patient.

The third example is that of a 48-year-old married male (Plate 6.3). His handling of Design 3, seemingly intact, has a significant space between the large angle and the next-inside, five-dot angle. The masked anger and the separation would suggest the possibility of rage reaction that is denied once controls are reinstituted. As a matter of fact, this man had been charged with aggravated assault and had had no reasonable explanation for his behavior once the rage subsided. The spacing of the diagram is of major significance; in particular, extra space between the frontal angles, often indicates the presence of intense, covert anger.

The fourth example of Design 3 is from a 19-year-old, single female (Plate 6.4). Not only are the dots regressed to circles, but there are an enormous number of extra dots in the front and second line. The rage in this woman was of phenomenal intensity, and the interpretation of this characteristic was confirmed in her refusal to come back to complete the testing even though her attorney believed that reevaluation was essential to her defense.

Plate 6.1
Card 3 by a 23-year-old Male

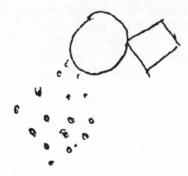

Plate 6.2
Card 3 by a 30-year-old Female

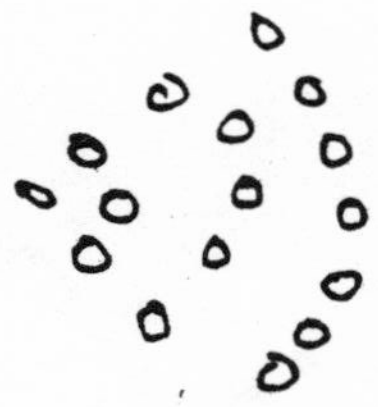

39

Plate 6.3
Card 3 by a 48-year-old Male

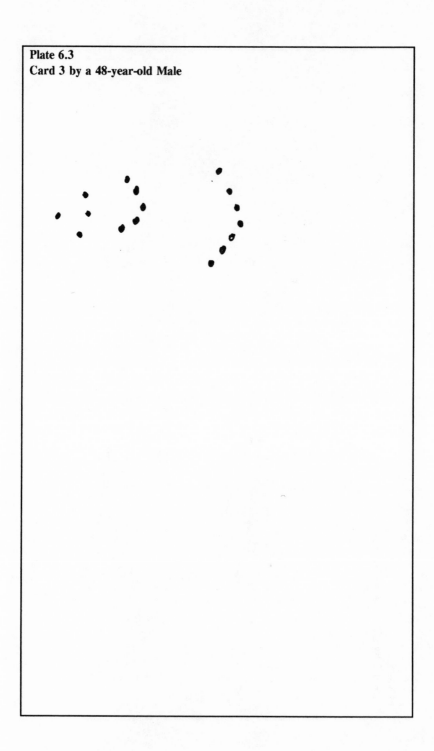

Plate 6.4
Card 3 by a 19-year-old Female

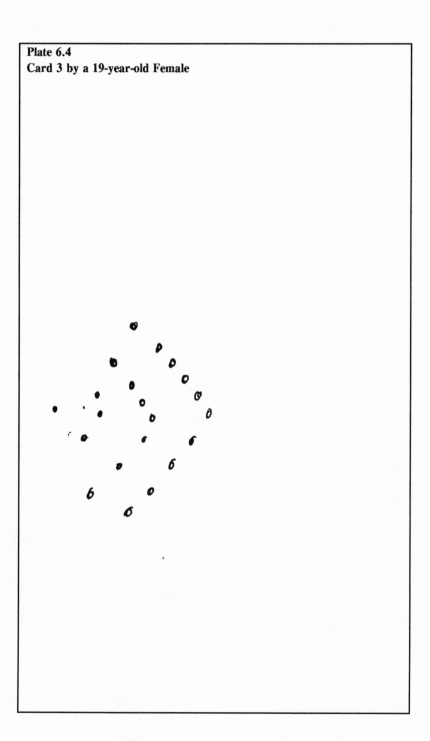

REVIEW QUESTIONS

1. This card measures

   a. penetration concerns.
   b. organicity.
   c. hostility.
   d. all of the above.

2. Men who draw open circles instead of dots

   a. are nurture-deprived.
   b. are enraged, often toward their fathers.
   c. combine sex with aggression.
   d. all of the above.

3. If the center or midline running through the arrow is not straight, consider

   a. epilepsy or organicity.
   b. depression.
   c. gross sexual turmoil.
   d. none of the above.

4. Women who erase and redraw this design smaller

   a. may have gross feelings of inadequacy.
   b. may be depressed.
   c. may have paranoid ideation.
   d. may have intense penetration anxiety.

Chapter 7

CARD 4

Chapter 7 involves an analysis of Card 4, described in our system as evaluating peer relations in particular and evaluating separation and individuation from parental figures in general. However, this latter interpretation must be used judiciously, as will be discussed. Generally speaking, the three-sided box is a symbolic representation of a male figure and the curved line is a symbolic representation of a female figure. Whichever figure is drawn larger by the patient is likely to be seen as the dominant sex.

A female who draws the female figure line noticeably larger than the male figure or overlaps the male figure with it is likely to dislike men, consciously or unconsciously, and may be prone to control or punish them verbally or physically. In such a case, the woman may have identified with an aggressive father, hiding identity confusion and anger with controlling, punitive behavior. Like their male counterparts, these women are often, pseudo seductive and sexually dysfunctional with men in terms of heterosexual orgasmic response. Histories of sexual abuse by older males is not uncommon. They sometimes accentuate their visible femininity to camouflage their identity confusion and self-loathing. It is valuable to note that the men involved with these women are often in a state of constant confusion and fear, due in part to the women's aggressiveness and inconsistency.

If the female figure drawn by a female is under or partially under the horizontal line of the male figure, she may be subservient and/or masochistic with either sex, but particularly with men. However, if the female figure is drawn nearer the right vertical side of the male figure, it is possible that she is intensely competitive and mistrustful of other women.

If the intensity of a woman's pencil stroke is greater (darker) on this card, as well as on Card A, she is seen as intensely angry and unable to maintain a subordinate role with anyone, regardless of the need felt for that relationship.

If the female figure line drawn by a male is overlapping the male figure box, the man usually feels, and is, dominated by female figures in general and is likely to perceive women as threatening. Avoidant, passive, and passive-aggressive interactions with females are commonly found in these males.

If the male figure box drawn by a male penetrates the female figure line, it is likely that he dislikes women and may seek to hurt them either verbally or physically. Also, if the right side of the male figure box is higher than the left side, it is likely that he uses a pseudo masculine, "macho" image or presentation with women, as if to suggest, "I'm in charge; you do what I say or I will punish you." Women involved with these men are at risk of verbal or physical abuse.

The darker the line men use to draw the box, the more likely these men are to be Don Juan types: pseudo masculine men who are deeply identity-confused, with a manifest need to prove their masculinity repetitively in accentuated, stereotypic, and aggressive ways. While often promiscuous to prove their masculinity, these men are also often homophobic, to convince themselves that they are not homosexually oriented.

Individuals of either sex who draw any separation between the two figures of this diagram are likely to have serious peer relationship disturbances, even if the separation between the figures is microscopic. These individuals are often mistrustful and may be overtly paranoid. Their relationships are usually superficial and often manipulative in nature. Alcohol, food, and drug addictions are often prevalent in individuals with disturbances of this type.

Individuals of either sex who draw the male area with rounded angles are likely to view males, particularly those who represent paternal figures, as possessing stereotypic feminine characteristics. For example, a blind analysis of a Bender reproduction drawn ten years earlier by a 13-year-old girl was conducted by one of the authors. The young girl had drawn the male area of Card 4 with accentuated round angles. The interpretation made by the author was that her father may have had overt or covert homosexual leanings. It was later revealed that in fact, her father had divorced her mother for his male lover some five years after the girl had been evaluated.

The first example of a distortion of Card 4 (Plate 7.1) is by a 48-year-old, twice-married male. In his reproduction of Card 4 he emphasizes the importance of the female design. The elaboration of the female figure line (shown as a double line) would suggest that constant turmoil and anger involving females was an integral part of his overall functioning. His hostility toward females would be interpreted from the penetration of the female symbol by the male symbol. The double extension of the female figure line, even though minimal, again suggests that the turmoil itself is on a lifelong basis, reflecting the macho needs of this extremely dependent individual. The faint horizontal line of the male figure would be interpreted as deep-seated masculine inadequacy. The darker vertical lines of the male figure serve to mask the self-esteem deficits with a pseudo masculine facade.

The second example (Plate 7.2) comes from a 27-year-old, twice-married, twice-divorced woman presently engaged to be married for a third time. The strongly elevated female portion of Card 4 appears to overwhelm the male portion and suggests that she is an extremely competitive and aggressive individual who very likely has identification disturbances that have never been dealt with effectively. In terms of her relationship with the parental figures, the father figure was seen as aggressive, and as stated above, Card 4 often reflects identification problems and difficulties. The aggressiveness in this woman suggests the need for psychotherapeutic involvement, but it is unlikely that she would tolerate giving up "control". The male figure in this design does not have squared angles, which in keeping with the elevated female figure, reflects a feminization of male figures. The elevated right side of the male figure emphasizes the identity confusion and aggressivity in this woman.

The third example comes from a 9-year, 4-month-old boy (Plate 7.3). The basis for his referral was his conscious and constant efforts to be controlling, particularly toward his mother. The major aspects involved his intense anger toward his 4-year old sister. His elaboration of Design 4 (the only elaborated design of the nine) via accentuated line endings reflects the center of the turmoil that is ongoing, and the capping of the points by emphasizing dot-like figures, suggests that this child was feeling nurture-deprived because the younger sibling was getting attention. In addition, the male figure is penetrating and flattening the female figure, and this would be in keeping with statements made previously about expressing aggression toward female figures. Of major significance is the finding that a severe distortion in terms of elaboration occurred only on Card 4, underlining the intense peer relationship disturbances. He was constantly challenging the authority of mother and his female teachers and was aggressive to the point of violence with several of his classmates.

The fourth example was obtained from a 14-year, 6-month-old girl (Plate 7.4). The indication of aggressiveness, as noted in the dislocation of the male symbol and its penetration of the female symbol of the card, was confirmed behaviorally, in that she had been convicted of aggravated assault in the stabbing of her own mother. The design suggests the rage involved, and the towering female portion of the design is in keeping with her acting-out behavior. The character-disorder functioning of this girl was seen throughout the protocol and confirmed in terms of her behavior; there was no noticeable test anxiety present in her casual reproduction of the Bender designs, and particularly in her uncritical reproduction of Design 4.

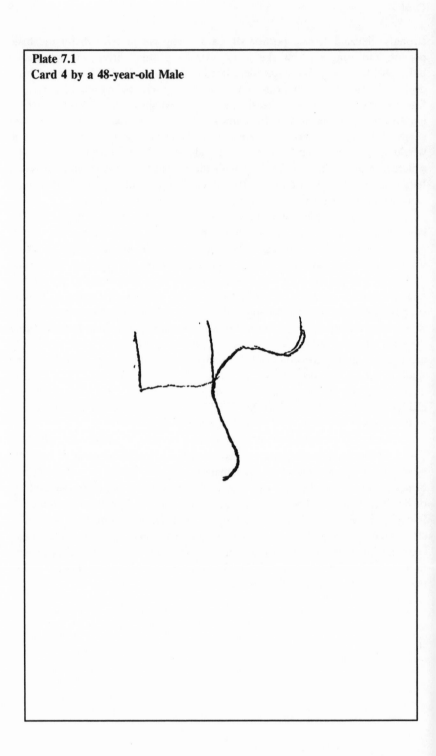

Plate 7.1
Card 4 by a 48-year-old Male

Plate 7.2
Card 4 by a 27-year-old Female

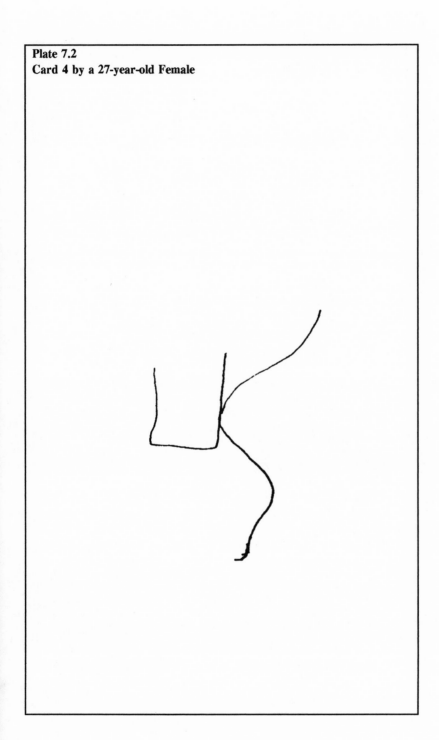

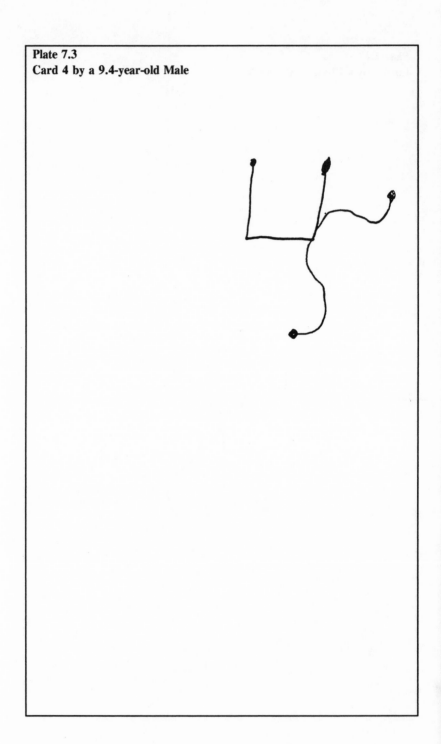

Plate 7.3
Card 4 by a 9.4-year-old Male

Plate 7.4
Card 4 by a 14.6-year-old Female

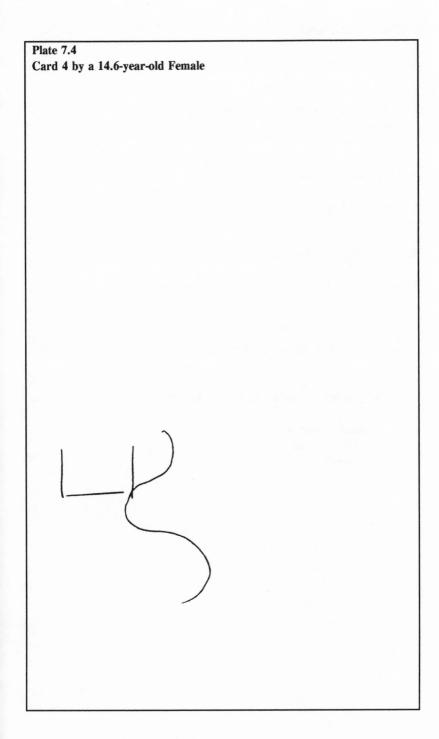

REVIEW QUESTIONS

1. If these two figures do not touch, the patient is

   a. depressed.
   b. unable to develop meaningful relationships.
   c. schizophrenic.
   d. all of the above.

2. The open box figure is

   a. a male symbol.
   b. a female symbol.
   c. neither (a) nor (b).
   d. either (a) or (b), depending on the sex of the patient.

3. If a male draws the curved figure under the open box, he is

   a. a malingerer.
   b. organically impaired.
   c. pseudo masculine and/or charismatic.
   d. mature.

4. If a female draws the curved figure overlapping the open box figure, she

   a. has paranoid ideations.
   b. is aggressive to males.
   c. is schizophrenic.
   d. all of the above.

Chapter 8

CARD 5

This diagram is considered a breast/penis figure and is useful in the assessment of exaggerated dependency and exaggerated sexual pressures. Card 5 can yield a great deal of information regarding the relationship of the individual taking the test with his or her mother figure in particular, and with females in general. If the individual taking the test is a female, the information regarding the involvement with mother in general and with males in particular also appears. The straight, angulated row of seven dots is the penis line; the semicircular configuration of dots is the breast area. Psychopathy, sociopathy, and underlying schizophrenia are frequently manifested in this diagram. The response reflects whether and how the patient copes with the onset of sexuality (puberty) and separation from the mother figure. This process heralds the loss of dependency on mother and father when puberty begins, usually around age 10.

If the first dot on the left of the breast figure is missing, the individual did not receive adequate bonding with or nurturance from the mother figure during much of the first year. Schizophrenia and/or manic depressive psychosis, as well as many other severe forms of psychopathology, should be considered. Also, counting from left to right on the breast figure, any greater-than-expected separation between the dots often reflects an approximate age (equal to the number of dots) at which separation from the mother figure was exacerbated and traumatic. Distortions in the breast figure frequently reflect difficulty with the important dependency relationship with nurturing figures, and regression from dots to circles is the most common distortion to emphasize the disturbance. Any open circles instead of dots reflect exacerbated dependency processes, like those associated with psychotic or psychopathic individuals. Proneness to drug, food, gambling and/or alcohol addiction should be considered whenever regression from dots to circles occurs.

The penis line should ideally intersect the breast area between the eleventh and twelfth dots (again counting from left to right). If this deviates from the model, the location may reveal the age at which the patient had trouble with the onset of puberty or possibly experienced a sexual trauma, including molestation.

If the penis line comes near or actually penetrates another diagram, then the possibility of psychosis, particularly schizophrenia, may be present and reflects the overwhelming libidinal pressure experienced by the patient. If the patient is male, consider the capacity for rape or murder accentuated. If the patient is female, sadomasochistic patterns are likely to be extensive. She is likely to be a penis-bearing, castrating, masculine woman. This is also true of females who draw less than seven dots in the penis line, thereby diminishing the length of the penis figure. Men who draw less than seven dots in the penis line generally tend to be ineffectual and passive and are often impotent. Their reductionist pattern suggests an overall lack of self-esteem, particularly in terms of sexual functioning.

If either or both aspects of the design are converted to straight lines rather than dots, consider conscious, exaggerated dependency needs at early childhood, pre-Oedipal levels, with frank, overt sexual avoidance. These individuals, often including anorexics, just want to be held and caressed, since their needs are at early, very primitive levels. Any form of adult sexual functioning is apt to overwhelm them, creating increased anxiety to the point of panic attacks (as often seen in all forms of phobic disorders).

The first example was obtained from a 17-year, 11-month-old male (Plate 8.1). Whereas all of his other designs were definitely separated from each other in reproduction, his Cards 5 and 6 collided. There is a significant variability in the quality of the dots leading up to the penis symbol (i.e., size, circles instead of dots, darkness) and a wider spacing following the inclusion of the penis line. The collision is gross (intellectually he would be capable of functioning in the superior range) and reflects his overwhelming anger and grossly distorted dependency needs. In fact, he had had significantly negative reactions to LSD and had been involved with drugs for a significant period of time. With respect to relationships, the sudden penetration of one figure into another allows a strong interpretation in terms of the dynamics involved.

The second example was obtained from a 12-year-old girl (Plate 8.2). The seemingly minimal distortion at the intersection of the male symbol with the female symbol indicated serious affective stress involving sexual trauma (confirmed in other measures and in the clinical material). The design reflects the regression in terms of circles instead of dots and, in addition, indicates anger both in terms of nurture deprivation and in terms of traumatic involvement with a male figure.

The third example (Plate 8.3) was obtained from the 14-year, 7-month-old boy seen in Chapters 3, 4, and 5 (Plates 3.3, 4.4, and 5.1), who had impairment stemming from organic deficit which was obvious in his overall Bender. Qualitatively, however, the severe regression to circles instead of dots reflects the impulsivity and the excessive demand for nurture in his interaction with parental figures. Behaviorally, he was constantly seeking attention, and his handling of Design 5 was emphatic in suggesting overwhelming impulsivity in his affective behavior. The joining of circles, the irregularity of the various internal aspects of the design, and the primitive configuration were all indicative of the overall impulse-ridden acting out behavior of this child.

The fourth example was obtained from a 21-year-old female (Plate 8.4). Her handling of Card 5 was again in terms of ruptured dependency pressures, and the displacement of the last dot (off the page) suggests that the disruption had come in the previous year or two of her life. Actually, she had been in a serious auto accident and was disfigured but would not accept plastic surgery. Additionally, the omission of the first dot in the breast figure (bottom left) supports serious nurture deprivation in the first year of life.

Her disproportionate handling of both aspects of Design 5 would be in keeping with the disruption in both dependency gratifications and libidinal gratifications. The ideation was pressuring this girl (the male symbol touches the top edge of the page), but the behavior was that of an isolated, constricted individual. Her handling of Card 5 was seen as a reflection of her ongoing emotional turmoil and disturbance.

The fifth example (Plate 8.5) was obtained from a 31-year-old alcoholic male who was unable to financially maintain himself and was being supported by his family. The complete penetration of Design 5 by Design 6 reflects the dangerous anger toward female figures, while the limited number of dots in the male area suggests his feelings of impotency and his overall passivity. The collision is, of course, interpreted as most collisions are; that is, as psychotic processes operating. It was of interest in dealing with this overall Bender that the first major disruption occurred in the handling of Cards 5 and 6. Whereas, the subject had the correct number of dots and circles in his earlier patterns, his dependency symbol was significantly different and was inaccurate in terms of configuration. In general, the greater the distortion obtained, the more credible and reliable is the interpretation made.

The sixth example (Plate 8.6) came from the 26-year-old female discussed in Chapter 5 (Plate 5.3). Her placement of the design with an almost 90-degree rotation would be interpreted in terms of distorted and deviant dependency needs, and this was readily confirmed in the clinical picture. This was an extremely bright individual holding a graduate degree, and Card 5 was one of two of her Bender designs that were seriously distorted. In both distortions, the affective disruptions were indicated and confirmed clinically. The unusual placement suggests an almost autistic handling of environmental factors; it also suggests that in emotional areas the turmoil would be intense.

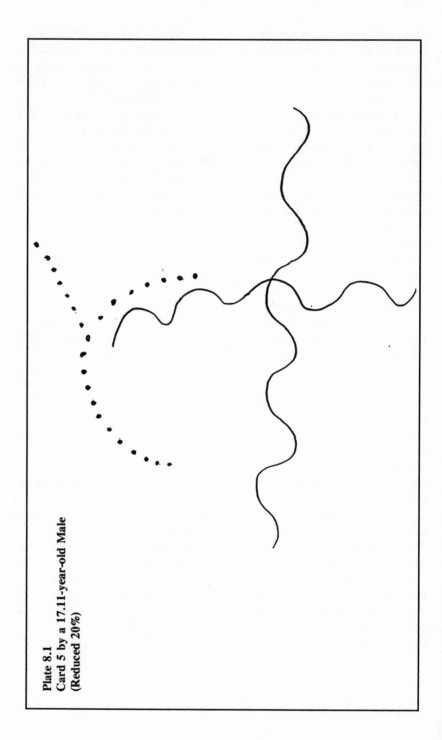

Plate 8.1
Card 5 by a 17.11-year-old Male
(Reduced 20%)

54

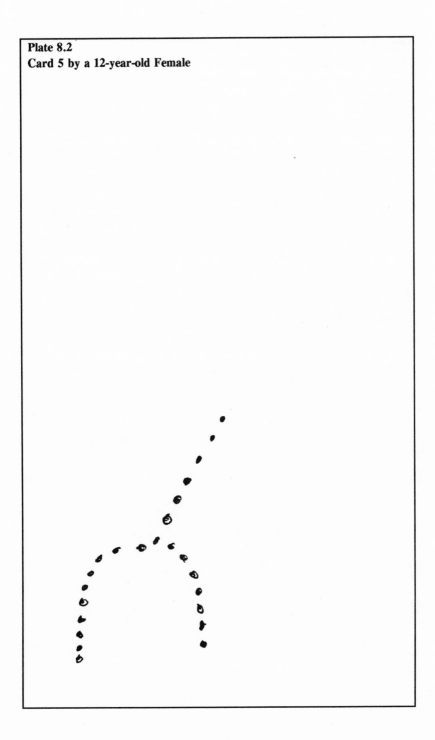

Plate 8.2
Card 5 by a 12-year-old Female

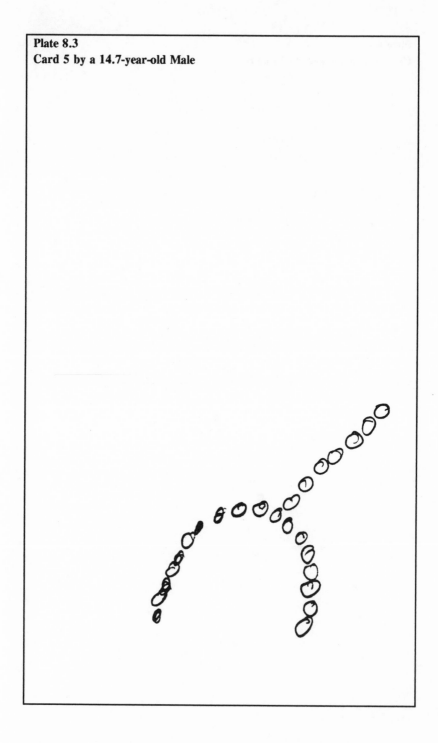

Plate 8.3
Card 5 by a 14.7-year-old Male

Plate 8.4
Card 5 by a 21-year-old Female

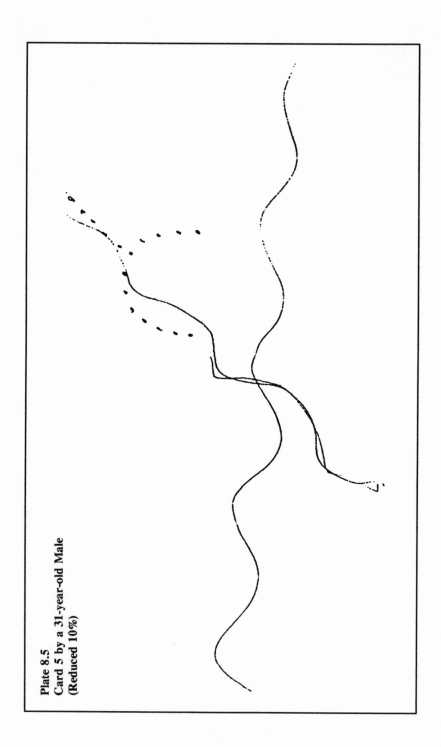

Plate 8.5
Card 5 by a 31-year-old Male
(Reduced 10%)

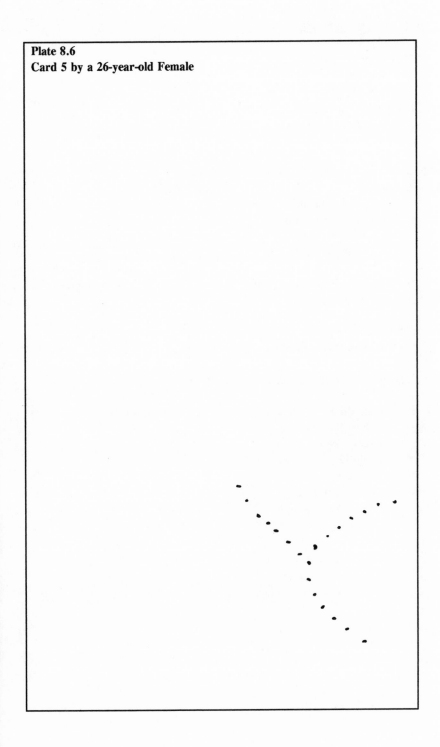

Plate 8.6
Card 5 by a 26-year-old Female

REVIEW QUESTIONS

1. This diagram assesses

   a. sexual needs.
   b. psychotic processes.
   c. dependency needs.
   d. all of the above.

2. Open circles instead of dots primarily reflect

   a. exacerbated dependency processes.
   b. poor peer relationships.
   c. sexual maturity.
   d. none of the above.

3. If the straight line of dots comes near or actually penetrates another diagram, consider

   a. bulimia.
   b. visual-motor retardation.
   c. schizophrenia.
   d. giving the patient another sheet of paper.

4. If a female draws six dots on the straight line of dots consider

   a. manic-depression.
   b. scoptophilia.
   c. schizophrenia.
   d. penetration anxiety.

Chapter 9

CARD 6

This diagram helps to assess overall types of disturbance involving both affect and hostility. The horizontal wavy line is used to measure affect in general and the handling of the subject's affect in particular. The vertical wavy line is used to measure anger, and of central importance is where and how the vertical line intersects with the affect line as compared to the model.

Generally, the two lines should intersect as they do in the model. If the hostility line (vertical) intersects the affect line to the right of center and below the affect line (out and down), one may consider indications of depression, psychotic processes, and schizophrenia. If the hostility line intersects the affect line to the right of the center and above the affect line (out and up), consider the possibility of a weakened superego and ego, and usually the protocol is that of acting out, as most often found in the severe character-disordered, psychopathic or sociopathic individuals. If the intersection of the hostility line is to the left of the center of the affect line and above (in and up), the individual is depressed, and intra-punitive pressures are likely to be present. Suicidal or homicidal acting out should be considered if other factors support this configuration.

If the hostility line intersects to the left of the center of the affect line and below it (in and down), the likelihood of exaggerated use of repression should be considered. In this case, the subject may be treating the objectionable impulse regarding sex or hostility as though it were nonexistent. These individuals often forget or repress to avoid these unpleasant situations. Histrionic or hysterical patients commonly tend to make this distortion as do individuals with dissociative tendencies who have exaggerated psychogenic disturbance in memory.

Of secondary importance is the quality of the lines, indicating which aspect is accentuated. The line pressure, as shown by the weight or darkness of the line, and the location of the stroke will suggest which affect is accentuated. Similarly, any breaks in the lines or other deviations in the line quality tend to reflect difficulties in control.

If any of the curves are pointed, organic impairment should be considered. The more pointed the curves, the greater the probability of organic neurological impairment. That is, rather than a smooth curve, the distortion is in terms of a series of points instead of curves.

If the hostility line comes close to or intersects with another diagram, indication as to a cause of the hostility is suggested. Also, one should always consider schizophrenia if the hostility line intersects another diagram. Similarly, if either line ends against any edge of the paper, serious consideration of psychotic processes is indicated. Of course, these severe disturbances will be either confirmed or ruled out by additional psychological tests and a mental status examination.

The first example (Plate 9.1) was obtained from the 26-year-old female who was the last example in the previous chapter. This was the individual with a graduate degree. The rapid, uncritical handling of this design, with the vertical line higher than it should be, reflects the gross affective turmoil and disturbance that was mentioned in dealing with her reproductions of Cards 2 and 5 (Plates 5.3 and 8.6).

Her handling of Card 6 reflects affective disruptions in the psychotic ranges. This particular design was done totally separate from all the other figures, in that no other design is on the page. The interpretation would be in terms of the severity of disturbance, since it was placed alone despite instructions not to put a single design on a page. While statements regarding the difficulty of this design are obtained frequently, the major distortion in this case appeared in terms of placement, rather than actual design distortion. Diminishing the size of both lines was her attempt to portray more control than she actually possessed. As stated earlier, the intersection of the two lines was out and up, suggesting excessively weakened superego and ego.

The second example (Plate 9.2) was obtained from a 14-year-old boy, who was struggling to maintain controls over disturbing affective ideation. As will be noted, the horizontal line was erased and redone, and the vertical line contains numerous small distortions. In addition, the vertical line was drawn lighter in terms of pencil stroke than the horizontal line. His greatest difficulty in duplicating the Bender designs came with this figure and reflected the ongoing stress and disturbance regarding demonstrations of affect. His handling of Card 6 was similar to his handling of the other Bender cards in terms of demonstrating the constriction and restriction involved in his affective functioning. The distortions in the lower portion of the vertical (hostility) line resemble small tail and suggest both intra-punitive and passive aggressive expression of his hostility.

The third example was obtained from a 16-year-old girl (Plate 9.3). The line quality of her Design 6 was significantly different from the line quality in any of her other Bender designs, and the horizontal line (affect) was the lightest of all the lines in her reproduction, suggesting the presence of primary process disturbance in affectively charged situations. She partially erased the hostility line and redrew it closer to the center of the affect line, emphasizing her exaggerated use of denial of her anger. The overt expression of anger is totally unacceptable to her. Her overwhelming concern with effective female role pressures was emphasized by her appearance. She wore a T-shirt with a Marine Corps logo, which in 1978 would have been considered excessively masculine for a girl of her age. The disturbances involving feelings were severe and mentioned consciously in terms of feeling "alone". The diminished size of both of her lines was her attempt to exhibit more control of her emotions than she actually possessed. She was a social recluse who had a history of emotional disturbance.

The fourth example was obtained from a 15-year, 5-month old girl (Plate 9.4). The sudden sharp upswing and flattening of the affect line suggests the acting-out of affective turmoil, and this was readily found both in her verbalization and in her test responses. She gave as problem areas "drugs, alcohol, and getting along with my parents". The loss of affective control was severe and had resulted in her hospitalization. In keeping with previous statements, the severity of the upsurge on the horizontal line leaves little doubt as to the interpretation regarding disruptive emotional functioning. The backward tilt and the darkening of the hostility line emphasize the pronounced negativism and hostile non-compliance.

The fifth example (Plate 9.5) was obtained from a 31-year-old male who was also discussed in the preceding chapter (Plate 8.5), due to the severe collision and penetration of Design 6 into Design 5. The line quality and size of Design 6 is exaggerated; the upper portion of the hostility line is far longer than the model, and along with the collision that was discussed, gross affective distortions and disturbances were seen, and the findings were consistent with all of the projective measures. The hostility towards females in general has reached psychotic levels and the subject should probably be considered extremely dangerous to women or girls. The downward tilt of the affect line accentuates an underlying depression and the overall design is suggestive of regression to schizophrenic functioning.

The sixth example was obtained from an 11-year-old boy and reflects his separation from others in terms of feelings (Plate 9.6). (His other designs in the Bender reproductions were in keeping with this, with the figures in Design 4 completely separated.) The length of the hostility line below the affect line suggests that denial and/or repression are exaggerated defense mechanisms for this child, and it emphasizes the need for psychotherapeutic help. He is fearful of acting out his anger, and he is trying desperately to maintain control by avoiding interacting with others. Confirmation of this appeared in other projective measures, and again the clinical picture provided validation for this interpretation. He had been referred for evaluation by the school administrator after repeated psychosomatic complaints that resulted in excessive school absenteeism.

The seventh example was obtained from a 23-year-old male (Plate 9.7). The reproduction of Card 6, with its right-hand side missing because his drawing was at the page's edge, combined with the excessive number of curves in the vertical line, was interpreted as showing potential danger in his overall affective functioning, and he was seen as in needing therapeutic help. He was an extremely angry individual who had been functioning ineffectively as a police trainee, and repeated demonstrations of poor judgment had resulted in his dismissal. The rage and anger that he lived with were a constant threat to his effective functioning, and one of the earliest signs in the psychological patterns was the sudden end of the affect line in the Bender.

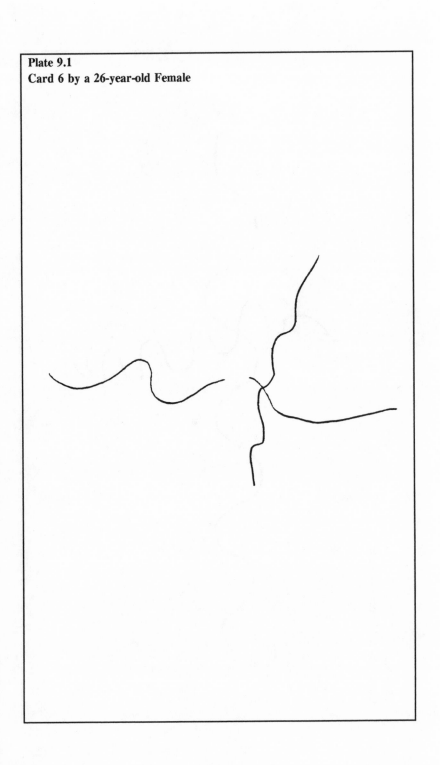

Plate 9.1
Card 6 by a 26-year-old Female

Plate 9.2
Card 6 by a 14-year-old Male

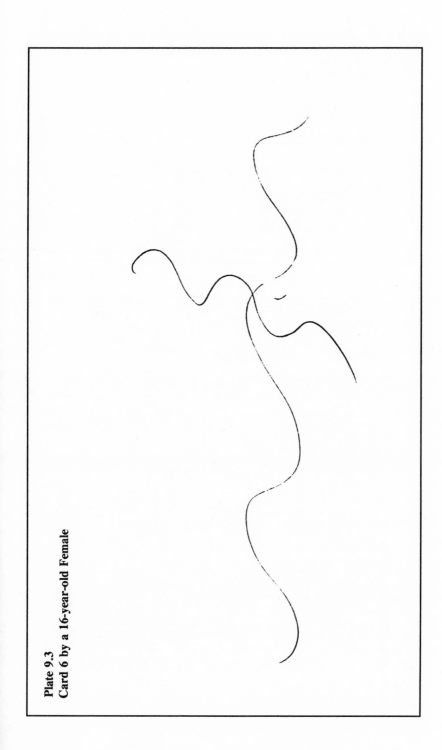

Plate 9.3
Card 6 by a 16-year-old Female

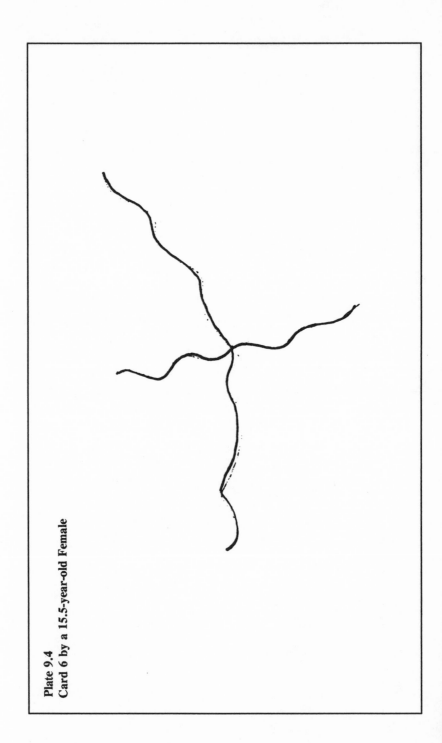

Plate 9.4
Card 6 by a 15.5-year-old Female

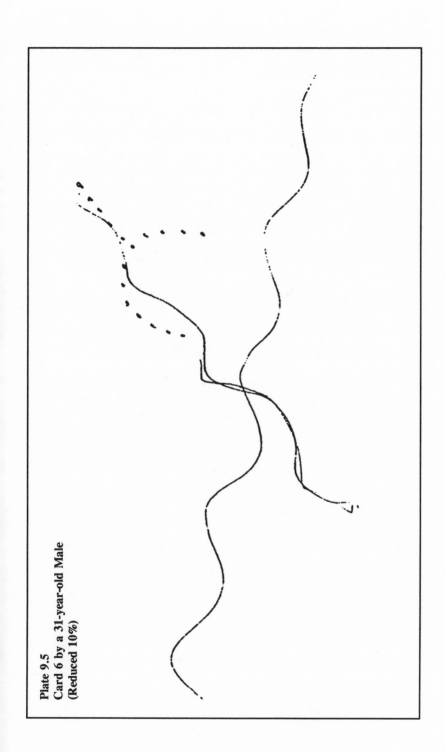

Plate 9.5
Card 6 by a 31-year-old Male
(Reduced 10%)

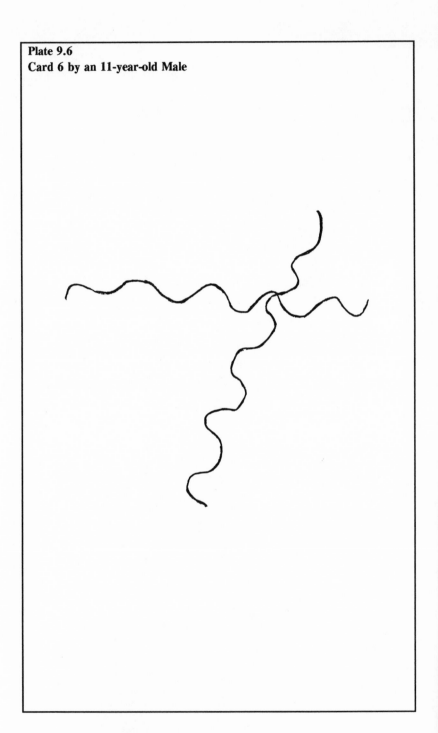

Plate 9.6
Card 6 by an 11-year-old Male

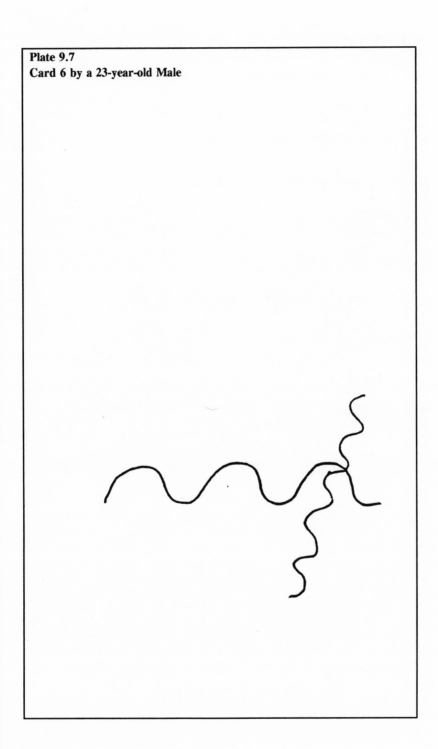

Plate 9.7
Card 6 by a 23-year-old Male

REVIEW QUESTIONS

1. The horizontal line measures

   a. ego strength.
   b. emotion or affect.
   c. superego lacunae.
   d. none of the above.

2. If any of the curves are pointed, consider

   a. compulsivity.
   b. sexual deviancy.
   c. organicity.
   d. none of the above.

3. If the vertical line intersects another design, consider

   a. psychotic process.
   b. organicity.
   c. bulimia.
   d. none of the above.

4. If the pressure of the pencil stroke of the vertical is significantly darker than the horizontal line, consider

   a. despair.
   b. panic.
   c. rage.
   d. exhilaration.

Chapter 10

CARD 7

Card 7 measures sexuality in older adolescents and adults. Children and young adolescents are not expected to have achieved psychosexual maturity and, therefore, interpretative data from this card with regard to sexuality are specific to individuals who have reached biologic, endocrinologic maturity. The card also provides another measure of neurological damage or organicity. First, we will address the interpretations of sexual function and dysfunction.

On this design, line quality is again important and instructive, especially where and how it deviates from the model. Faint lines reflect sexual avoidance and/or feelings of sexual inadequacy. This usually implies immaturity and a prepubescent psychosexual fixation. In addition, broken lines qualitatively reflect disruptions of sexual ideation into consciousness and/or disruptions in sexual functioning.

Darkened lines may be indicative of aggressive and/or sadistic tendencies wherein sex and aggression have merged. Lines darkened or extra sharp at the points also reflect anger expressed in sexual behavior (i.e., sexual battery). Males who accentuate the points in this manner may be excessively aggressive to women. Conversely, women who accentuate the points in this manner may be excessively aggressive to men. Any inconsistency in the line quality may reflect sexual trauma. An erasure on this diagram raises the question of penetration anxiety by either sex. Excessive erasures usually reflect gross sexual turmoil.

If the figures do not overlap, or overlap insufficiently, castration anxiety in males and penetration anxiety in females is likely and sexual fear is overwhelming. Similarly, if the figures overlap excessively, the individual is preoccupied with libidinal ideation and the possibility of primary process (schizophrenia) should be considered for either sex.

The relationship of the size of the model to the duplication made by the patient is significant. If the figures are significantly smaller than the model, sexual functioning and/or sexual ideation may be seen as threatening. If they are significantly larger, the libidinal (sexual) pressures are correspondingly intense and sexual acting out may be likely.

Where this design is drawn in relation to others is also quite important. If it overlaps or comes close to any other design, the possibility of sexual deviancy and/or schizophrenia should be considered. As with Card 3, if the figures are drawn, then erased and redrawn smaller than the model, severe penetration or castration concerns are likely.

Occasionally this design is placed on a separate page from Designs 1 through 6. This separation reflects intense anxiety generated by the sexual nature of this design and should be considered another indication of psychosexual immaturity and resulting avoidance of sexual ideations.

Neurologically, separations, breaks in the line quality or rounded corners on these figures are often seen in individuals with frontal lobe damage. The absence of these distortions would be a contraindication for organic damage. Of course, many other plus signs must be present before a confirmation of neurologic damage is made and it should be kept in mind that distortions in dealing with this design are not necessarily organic. It may be necessary, if the clinician considers it important, to ask for a repeat of the design to see if it can be improved enough to negate the interpretations considered as a result of the initial reproduction.

The first example was obtained from an 18-year-old girl (Plate 10.1). Her reproduction of Design 7 has extremely sharp and darkened points on the left half of the figure, and a dagger-like quality is evident. The inconsistent, faint line quality also suggests sexual inadequacy and avoidance of sexual functioning. Trauma involved in sexual functioning was indicated in the Bender, and a follow-up confirmed the presence of sexual trauma. The difference in line quality between this design and all of her other designs reemphasized the likelihood that this was an accurate way of interpreting her reproduction. She had been molested several years earlier and had never told anyone.

The second example was obtained from a 13-year-old boy (Plate 10.2). Not only was this figure the smallest of all his Bender designs in terms of reproduction, but it contained repeated pencil tracings over the line, in keeping with the severe and psychotic functioning that the child was undergoing. (He had been hospitalized.) The difference in line quality, the difference in size, and the placement were all considered in terms of interpretation, and the findings of sexual turmoil of pathological proportions were confirmed in the clinical material.

The third example (Plate 10.3) was obtained from the 48-year-old male previously seen in Chapter 7 (Plate 7.1). His handling of Card 7, with enlarged figures, heavy line quality and the difference in intensity as compared with his other figures, all suggested an identification with an aggressive male and aggressive male sexual functioning for this individual. It further suggested the possibility that he could be dangerous, particularly toward women.

The fourth example was obtained from a 21-year-old female (Plate 10.4). The diminished separation and difference in proportion in both halves of her figure indicated the possibility of withdrawal and isolation in sexual areas. The repeated breaks in the lines were not organic indicators; rather, they reflected repetitive, gross sexual ideation that increased her isolation. The clinical material was in agreement with this finding. The sexual turmoil was intense, and psychotherapy would be essential if she was to function in an adult capacity.

The fifth example was obtained from a 15-year-old girl (Plate 10.5). The significant separation of all angles from the parallel lines was seen as indicating sexual aversion or serious negative reaction to libidinal ideation. The disturbances in sexual functioning were intense, and this individual repeatedly permitted herself to be "used," sexually and otherwise, by individuals in order to gain affective nurturance and attention. The disturbance in ideation, however, was intense, and the depression that resulted from the self-degrading functioning had become life-threatening for her.

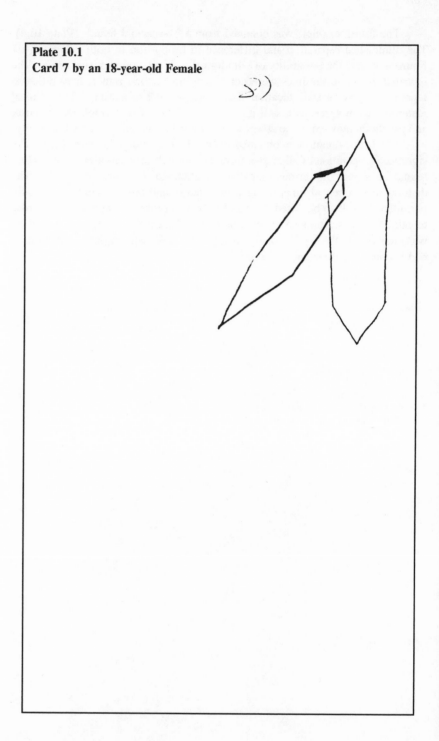

Plate 10.1
Card 7 by an 18-year-old Female

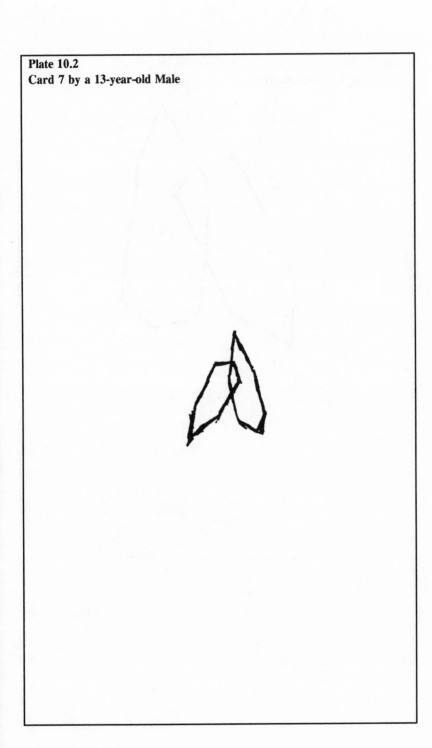

Plate 10.2
Card 7 by a 13-year-old Male

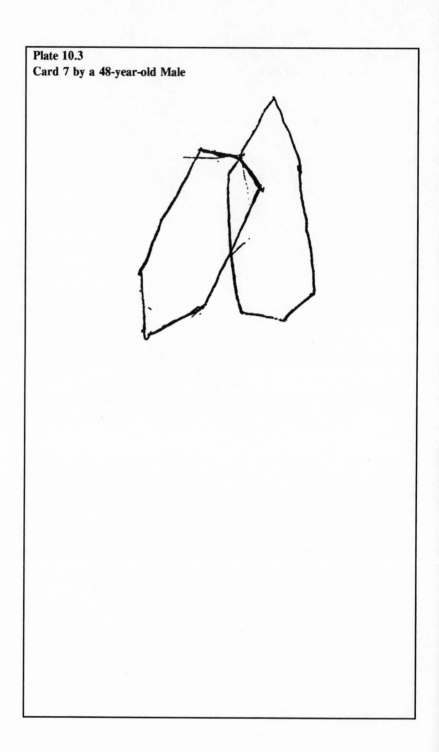

Plate 10.3
Card 7 by a 48-year-old Male

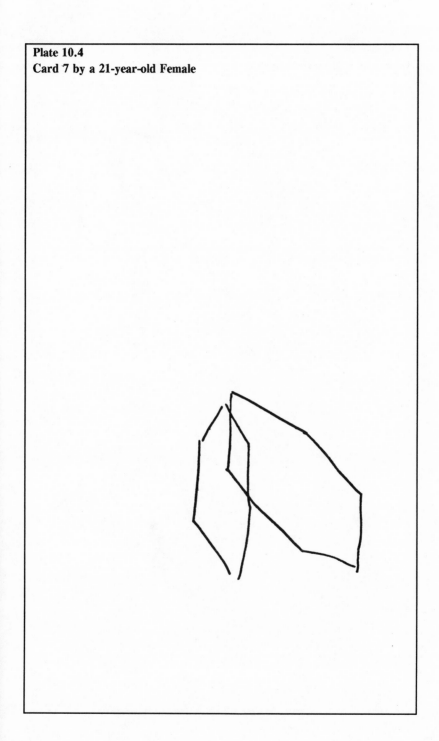

Plate 10.4
Card 7 by a 21-year-old Female

Plate 10.5
Card 7 by a 15-year-old Female

REVIEW QUESTIONS

1. This design measures

    a. both depression and sexuality.
    b. both organicity and sexuality.
    c. both organicity and depression.
    d. none of the above.

2. Excessive erasures on this design usually indicate

    a. affective pressures.
    b. sexual turmoil.
    c. organic damage.
    d. none of the above.

3. If this figure is drawn much smaller than the model,

    a. organic damage is severe.
    b. anger is overwhelming.
    c. sexual activity is high.
    d. sexual contact is threatening.

4. Darkened lines at the points or extra sharp points reflect

    a. anger expressed sexually.
    b. anxiety somatized.
    c. bipolar pressures.
    d. none of the above.

Chapter 11

CARD 8

This last card depicts psychosexual maturity. The center diamond may be interpreted as a vagina symbol while the outer shape is viewed as a penis symbol. As described in Chapter 10, the patient's chronological age must be considered when interpreting this design. Much of the following is most applicable to adolescents and adults. As with all previous cards, line quality is very important. Faint lines drawn by either gender reflect fears of intercourse or penetration in general; broken lines reflect serious sexual turmoil and possible trauma. The same findings are true if any heavy shading of the lines is seen. Darkened points when compared to the line weight of the rest of the drawing suggest some degree of merger between sex and aggression, as was mentioned on Card 7. Wavy or curved lines in the penis symbol reflect low frustration tolerance in general and self-denigrating feelings, particularly if the patient is male.

If the outer shape is much smaller than the model and drawn by a female, consider conscious dislike of heterosexual activity and/or a sexual identity disturbance. Smaller designs drawn by males often reflect inadequacy concerns, with sexual dysfunction likely (e.g., premature ejaculation and/or impotence).

If, when drawn by a female, the center diamond extends beyond the lines of the penis symbol, fear of heterosexual behavior or sexual anhedonia is likely. The greater the extension outside the boundaries of the outer shape, the greater is the fear of heterosexuality and the more pronounced is the sexual denial (often seen in the responses of exceedingly religiously oriented individuals). Only once in the authors' thirty years of testing experience was the "vagina" diamond completely ommitted from the reproduction. This was done by a female who was extremely asexual. She was a nun who had had a traumatic sexual history before adolescence.

If the entire figure is excessively larger than the model, consider sexual preoccupation with the possibility of schizophrenic processes operating. The latter interpretation is also very likely if the figure intersects or collides with any other figure. Even if organic indicators (Koppitz, 1963, 1975; Lacks, 1984; etc.) are present in this figure or in any of the others, the presence of psychodynamic indicators should be interpreted as well. The handling of this particular design is of major significance in dealing with sexual ideation/sexual fantasy and actual sexual functioning. The relationship of this design with the other designs will be discussed in Chapter 12.

The first example (Plate 11.1) was obtained from the 48-year-old male whose handling of Cards 4 and 7 (Plates 7.1 and 10.3) were discussed in detail. The reason for inclusion of Card 8 is the repeated likelihood of sexual aggression as a main concern with this individual. The exaggerated points on the line are consistent with threats made by this patient toward females, as confirmed by clinical findings. The pin-like extension on the tip of the left point would strongly support an interpretation of sexual inadequacy masked by acting-out sexual aggression. In addition to the pointed ends, the center diamond figure is drawn with heavier lines than the two faint parallel lines. Moreover, the points do not meet the parallel lines effectively and the interpretation of severe aggressive ideation would be enhanced.

The second example (Plate 11.2) was obtained from the 14.7-year-old male whose reproductions of Cards A, 1, 2, and 5 were previously addressed (Plates 3.3, 4.4, 5.1, and 8.3). In addition to the organic factors indicated in this reproduction, the extreme lengthening of the penis symbol and the exaggeration of the points is again seen as indicating severe aggressive ideation involving sexual functioning. The separation on the right point and the extension on the upper point of the vagina symbol through the penis line further supports the interpretation of a fusion between sex and aggression often noted in psychopathic sex offenders. The difficulty, aside from the reduced controls resulting from organic factors, reflects the overwhelming early adolescent turmoil for this child.

The third example (plate 11.3) was obtained from the 14-year-old boy previously discussed in Chapter 9 (Plate 9.2). The small size of the reproduction of Design 8 and the repeated, darkened lines in dealing with the points and the entire design would all consistently reflect the severely pathological ideation regarding sexual functioning and the covert fear of being ineffective in masculine functioning. His handling of Card 8 was consistent with the other indications of gross turmoil regarding affective interactions with others, particularly females, and served as a reason for his hospitalization.

The fourth example (Plate 11.4) was obtained from a 16-year-old female whose handling of Card 6 was discussed in Chapter 9 (Plate 9.3). Her significantly longer reproduction of Card 8 was seen as reflecting grossly disturbing libidinal ideation and sexual functioning, and this was confirmed in the clinical material. This design is larger than any of her other designs and she is the same individual who handled affect in Design 6 (Plate 9.3) with great difficulty. The extension of the lower point of the center diamond in conjunction with the extreme lengthening of the outer shape reconfirms the interpretation of primary process ideation and severely disturbed sexual functioning. The self-derogatory aspects of her Bender reproductions suggested the need for psychotherapeutic intervention. The disturbances mentioned in regard to Card 8 were confirmed and found repeatedly in the other personality measures.

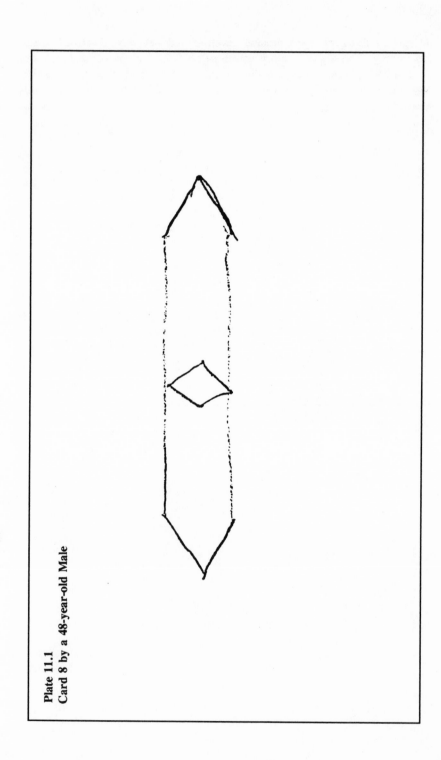

Plate 11.1
Card 8 by a 48-year-old Male

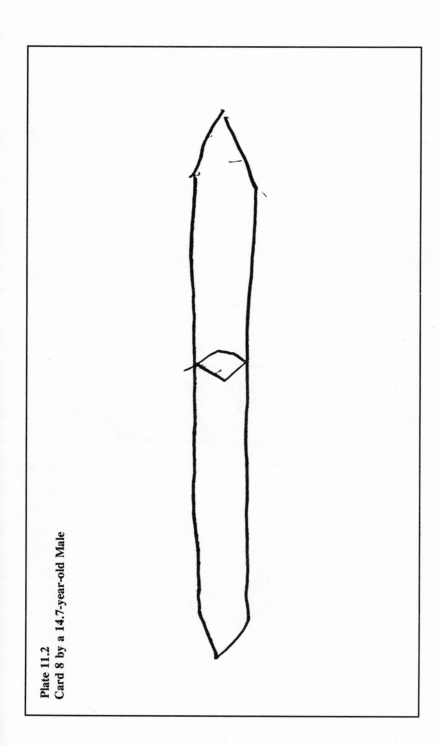

Plate 11.2
Card 8 by a 14.7-year-old Male

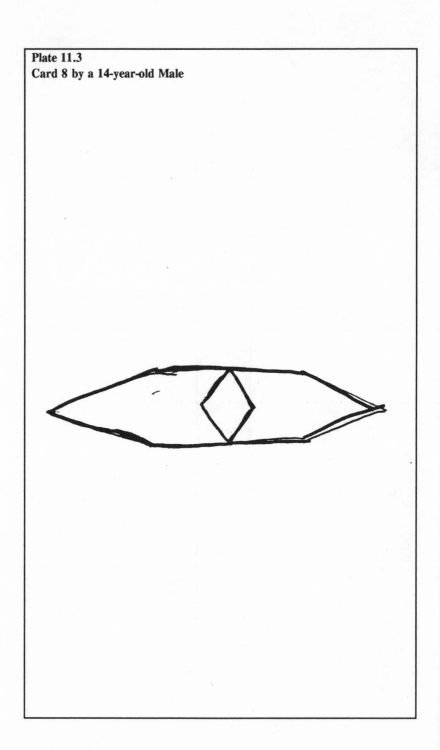

Plate 11.3
Card 8 by a 14-year-old Male

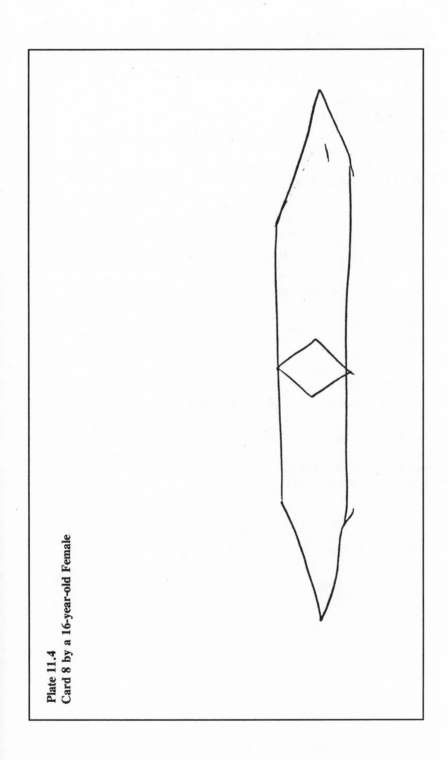

Plate 11.4
Card 8 by a 16-year-old Female

REVIEW QUESTIONS

1. The center box or diamond is

    a. a father symbol.
    b. an anger symbol.
    c. a mother symbol.
    d. a vagina symbol.

2. Faint lines on this design reflect

    a. organic damage.
    b. schizophrenia.
    c. dysphoric trends.
    d. none of the above.

3. If this design is drawn excessively larger than the model, consider

    a. schizophrenia.
    b. organicity.
    c. multiplicity.
    d. none of the above.

4. If this figure intersects another figure, consider

    a. schizophrenia.
    b. multiplicity.
    c. narcissistic personality.
    d. post traumatic stress disorder.

Chapter 12

THE INTERRELATIONSHIPS
AMONG THE DESIGNS

The purpose of the foregoing chapters was to provide specific psychodiagnostic indicators regarding individual responses to each of the Bender cards. In addition to the reproductions of each independent design, the relationships *among* the reproductions of the nine Bender cards are to be interpreted. This interrelationship within the Bender provides essential information and also helps in terms of analyzing the interrelationships between the Bender and other personality measures.

This chapter will contain a variety of complete Bender Gestalt protocols, including several from individuals who were discussed in previous chapters. The selections that follow were chosen because of the subtle rather than gross distortions they show, so that the importance of the indications found in the reproductions can be appreciated.

An identically duplicated series of Bender designs is highly unlikely. In our experience (over twenty thousand profiles), no two people have reproduced the designs in an identical way. The subtle variations that have been described in dealing with these cards provide a great deal of important information regarding the individual's dynamics. Of major importance is the "telling," in symbol and representation, of what may be disturbing to the individual and not in awareness. The reproductions provide a basis for giving the examiner information that derives from covert, unconscious pressures rather than just conscious productions.

The simplicity of the Bender, as has been indicated by others (e.g., Hutt, 1969), permits almost immediate indication of possible malingering or gross lack of self-criticalness. The designs, particularly for very bright people, create difficulty in terms of conscious attempts to demonstrate disturbance when knowledge concerning the designs is not available.

It is extremely difficult for most people to surmise what distortions would be necessary to demonstrate particular disabilities. Malingerers are usually confused and trapped by the relative simplicity of the designs to be reproduced. For example, while people with organic damage, especially congenital retardates, usually cannot make a diamond, more recent neurologic damage (i.e., from illness or trauma) may result in a fairly acceptable diamond. In the latter case, organic distortions will appear on Designs 3, 7, and 8. Another indication of malingering is seriously distorted designs regardless of the level of difficulty, but with no overlapping or collisions. This is often noted in personal injury litigation cases where the distortions are extreme but the designs are neatly drawn and sequentially placed on the paper. This involves a surprising degree of organization, in terms of placement, for someone who is appearing to be seriously disorganized and disoriented.   Also, the productions made by malingerers will be organized consistently from top to bottom or left to right or both. True organics, however, given the same instructions, will often show disarray in order. A visual example of this inherent organizational process can be found in Bender (1928, p. 151, plates 70 and 71), where the conscious distortions, deliberately made in order to show reduced effectiveness, demonstrated instead the subject's still-present organizational strengths in terms of the careful ordering and separation of the individual designs. For the most part, malingerers prefer verbal interaction to the Bender Gestalt Test and other projective tests, over which they feel less control.

It is interesting to note that even experimental subjects who try to trace each design by placing a piece of paper over the original do not provide exact reproductions. The pencil pressure, the selection of the space on the paper, the erasures, and the errors made can be extremely useful, particularly since the individual is not aware of what he or she is "saying" with the reproductions.

We have sometimes found it useful to ask for repeats, either of individual designs or of the entire series of Bender cards, at the end of a testing session. This may be done if the examiner feels that the initial reproductions were casually and uncritically done and if the examiner is faced with the possible interpretation of "organic" deficit.   A repeat, at least of the individual design in question, will eliminate or confirm the possibility of "organic" damage. Designs 3, 7, and 8 are extremely useful in determining organicity and should be repeated if "organicity" appears possible. As might be expected, the true organic can improve, at best, only slightly, and the impulsive, uncritical individual, if asked to repeat a design, usually shows marked improvement. It should also be remembered that asking for a repeat Bender can be seen as implied criticism; the corresponding anger in the individual may result in heavier pencil pressure, for example.

If more than one testing session is scheduled, then the possibility of the entire Bender being repeated at the end of the second session should be considered.   One of the benefits of the BGT is that this can be accomplished very quickly. A repeat of the entire Bender provides additional information in terms of the individual's reaction to the testing in general; that is, test anxiety should have been reduced by the time a second Bender is obtained, and the intra-design changes provide even more information regarding dynamics.

An additional advantage of a repeat Bender, in our experience, is that identical distortions on both trials enhance the likelihood that these errors reflect genuine representations of unconscious, premorbid functioning. While this is not always the case, it seems to be so in a vast majority of examples. However, since our assumption is that there can be no exact duplication of the designs and that individual variations occur at all times, interpretations on repeat Benders should be handled judiciously and at the discretion of the individual clinician.

Several examples of the effect and possible interpretation of the interrelation of the designs are shown in Plates 12.1 through 12.6 and the following analyses.

The first example (Plate 12.1) is of the reproductions by a 15-year-old boy, who gave as problem areas "getting excellent grades in school; accomplishing tasks (completing them)." As can be observed, each of the Bender designs is reproduced with effectiveness in terms of form quality. The major source of interpretation in terms of dynamics comes from his inversion of some of the designs (Cards A, 3, and 4), rotations (Cards 5 and 7), right-hand placement of the designs, and minimal distortions. The inversion and rotation of the designs and their placement at the right-hand side of the page, moving toward the left, reflects the overwhelming negativism and rebelliousness in this boy. In addition, the right-edge placement emphasizes the ongoing depression, which requires psychotherapeutic intervention.

It is obvious from the reproductions that this boy is a very bright, capable child who is not functioning effectively in the school setting. In addition to the overall significance of the design placements were the subtle indications of ongoing depression as seen in his individual reproductions. For example, Design 2 has a repetition of the first dot; Design 6 has an artificial emphasis of the affect line. The rotation of Design 5 emphasizes extreme negativism, and his upward sweep and erasure of the vertical line, the hostility symbol, serves to emphasize the anger and turmoil that he is trying to deal with in an ineffective, obsessive-compulsive fashion. Design 5 has variation in the dot formation, suggesting that he is experiencing what he feels as nurture loss; in addition, he rotated the design in keeping with his negativism. The vertical line of Design 6 turns toward the penis symbol area of Card 5, suggesting that the anger is directed more toward the father than toward the mother. A further possible interpretation that would have to be worked out with the other projective measures is the intense concern with the adult male role demands that are increasing for this adolescent. Designs 7 and 8 are more heavily duplicated than his other designs, and 8 is elongated. The center diamond in 8 is open-ended and is in keeping with his concern about increasing libidinal pressures, particularly toward females.

While these interpretations seem to be based on minimal distortions, it must be remembered that the clinical validity has extended over many years. In this example, the reversal of the arrow would further validate the intense, ongoing anger in this child, as well as the libidinal turmoil that is threatening his defenses and diminishing his ability to function both academically and interpersonally.

It is readily evident that this is an overly organized and integrated individual; there are no suggestions of organic deficit and no clear-cut indications of psychotic functioning. In the final analysis, where his other projective responses appeared, the above interpretations were confirmed. This was also found in terms of the clinical material that was later made available.

In the second example, the Bender reproductions of a hospitalized 16-year, 2-month old girl (Plate 12.2a) were compared to those of the same girl at 16-years, 11-months, while still in the hospital (Plate 12.2b). The first set of Bender designs is generally within acceptable limits in terms of form quality, but the diagnostic significance of Design 2, sweeping up toward the control line, is of major significance. The emphasis of the male figure in Design 4 reflects overwhelming libidinal turmoil, and the exaggerated upsweep of the affect line in Design 6 reflects her overall inability to maintain effective control over affective impulses. The disturbances were intense enough to require hospitalization and treatment.

In her later set of reproductions, the separation of each design with lines represents her attempt to maintain "logic-tight compartments," but these prove to be ineffective, since the distortions are still present. Significantly, Design 2 was not completed. Her reproduction consisted of eight series of three circles paired up, suggesting reduced effectiveness in maintaining controls even after the long hospitalization. The intense depression in this individual was reflected in her inability to complete Design 2. The extremely faint reproduction of the female portion of the peer relationship symbol, Card 4, and the grossly distorted and inaccurate reproduction of Card 6 (where in contrast with the gross upsurge of her reproduction at 16 years, 2 months, the present reproduction is down), indicates intense, ongoing depression. The libidinal turmoil can also be seen in Designs 7 and 8, where the line quality is heavy, particularly on the pointed ends of Card 8 and in the female symbol on Card 8. Of major importance is the significant difference in the handling of Card 6, where the pencil pressure on the dependency symbol indicators becomes lighter and lighter, in keeping with her constant concern with being "wanted." Each Bender performance was confirmed with the balance of the projective testing and clinical findings. The changes that occurred between the first testing and the second were also validated clinically.

The third example reflects the Bender configuration of a 7-year old male child (Plate 12.3). This protocol was received by one of the authors as a "blind" Bender to examine this author's effectiveness in dealing with psychological tests, particularly the Bender. The reproductions were made many years ago, and the child's history had been followed by the source due to the gravity of the circumstances therein. The author was asked to make an evaluation solely from the child's Bender reproductions; his age and sex, but no other identifying characteristics or history were given. After reviewing the reproductions, the author suggested that without psychotherapeutic intervention this child could be dangerous, particularly to females, as the libidinal pressures upon this individual intensified in early adolescence.

Overwhelming emotional disturbances appear in terms of the boy's use of the top edge of the page and failure to complete Designs 2 and 4. The conscious affect and the male symbol that was castrated in the reproduction of Design 4 reflect the anger, particularly toward the mother figure. The increased pencil pressure in Design 8, in terms of both the anger and the aggression toward female figures, was again emphasized. The arrow gives further indication of anger, as does the vertical hostility symbol in Card 6. The initial overall impression was that of a severely disturbed, potentially dangerous child, whose anger toward mother appeared to represent a real threat.

Of significance for this youngster is the extension underneath the mother figure symbol in Card A, which is interpreted as a penis symbol, indicating that the mother was extremely masculine, dominating, and aggressive. Although the father figure was elevated, reflecting the psychological parenting of the father figure, it is likely that the father's passivity was a factor in this boy's development. It was hypothesized that he had very little respect or use for either parent. His handling of Card 2 indicated a tenuous control of impulses, with a moderate to severe depression. Although he had some capacity to self-correct, his impulse controls were extremely primitive, and he was likely to lose the controls in an affective situation. His anger was increasing. The severe distortion of Card 2 was interpreted in terms of schizophrenia and acting out with no guilt or remorse. He had extreme difficulty in maintaining controls and could be a developing psychopathic schizophrenic. The treatment of Card 3 reflects both organic damage and gross sexual turmoil. It is likely that he was already confused between sex and aggression, and it was hypothesized that with the onset of puberty he would become very dangerous to females.

The treatment of Card 4, the peer relationship card, indicated that he was a socially isolated loner, with very little interest in or empathy for peer relationships. He viewed father as passive and feminine, as seen in the curvature in the masculine shape, and mother as dominant and withdrawn. He seems to have had little awareness of his parents as separate figures, and the wide gap between the two figures reflects, additionally, a deep disturbance in nurture, which was apparently interrupted often.

His response to Card 5, particularly the separation between the first and second dots on the breast area, indicates inadequate bonding in early infancy and exacerbated separation from mother at the earliest ages. His distortion of dots drawn as dashes in the penis figure on Card 5 was interpreted as overwhelming libidinal pressure. The capacity for dangerous acting-out behavior, confusing sex with aggression, was accentuated and increasing with age. The omission of the seventh dot in the penis line is interpreted in terms of castration fears and overall self-concept deficits.

Cards 6, 7, and 8 are handled in terms of intense aggression and threat, particularly to female figures. Since he was only 7 at the time of these Bender reproductions, the child's potential for dangerous acting-out behavior toward females would be considered extreme and would have to be dealt with if any accurate appraisal of his need for treatment were to be considered.

The examiner's evaluative capabilities with the Bender turned out to be frighteningly accurate. In actuality, this boy was accused and convicted of premeditated matricide in early adolescence.

The fourth example was done by a 37-year-old male charged with sexual battery (Plate 12.4). The offender was consistent in his concern with masculinity both in terms of the emphasized male area of Design 4 and in terms of the distortions on Designs 7 and 8. In addition, the affect line is flattened, and the expression of hostility by this man is made in covert, devious ways. The hostility line points to the left in his reproduction of Card 7. Dependency on mother and fear of women is overwhelmingly emphasized, which would be in keeping with the actual charge of child molestation. He was found guilty and sent to prison. Early in his examination, the Bender gave indications of his areas of turmoil and disturbance, and the balance of the projective measures confirmed these.

The fifth example (Plate 12.5) was obtained from a 30-year-old woman, who was discussed earlier in relation to her reproduction of Card 3 (Plate 6.2). The overall constriction and collisions of her reproductions suggest that gross ideational disturbances are present. The separation of Design A in terms of a nonnurturing mother and a hostile, absent father was confirmed clinically. The artificial restriction and the collisions suggest that she is basically an impulse-ridden, extremely angry individual who is not in control of her behavior, as seen in her regression to circles instead of dots on Card 3. In actuality, she had been arrested for setting fire to a building and was undergoing psychological evaluation in jail while awaiting trial that crime.

The relationships among the designs in this woman's Bender give many indications of the degree of disturbance and the focus point of her turmoil, particularly with parental figures. The penetration of Card 7 into the breast area of Card 5 and the projection of the male area on Design 5 almost to Design 2, as well as the regression to circles instead of dots on Designs 1 and 3, all emphasize possible ongoing psychotic processes in an individual capable of dangerous acting-out behavior. (She was later convicted of arson.)

The handling of the peer relationship symbol, particularly the female symbol, suggests that she tends to be submissive and passive in her heterosexual relationships. The extension of the father symbol (Card A) into the affect symbol (Card 2) and the diminished, castrated penis symbol (Card 5) raise the possibility of early molestation, but this was not confirmed clinically.

The sixth example was obtained from a 29-year-old male (Plate 12.6). The overall Bender protocol is of particular significance for two major reasons. The careful duplication, done in heavy pencil markings, suggests an almost desperate, unsuccessful effort to maintain control over his affect. In addition, the remarkable reduction in the size of the design when dealing with Card 4 (peer relationships) suggests that he had overwhelming conflicts regarding masculine functioning and was resorting to obsessive-compulsive defenses against unacceptable libidinal pressures. He had suffered a breakdown requiring hospitalization while in the armed services and, following his discharge from service, was hospitalized a second time. He appeared to be a deliberate, fragile, obsessive-compulsive individual in not only the Bender, but all of his test reproductions, but his attempts to function in a constricted fashion failed under pressure and he then engaged in antisocial behavior. The relationship aspect of the Bender in this series of reproductions emphasized the need for psychotherapeutic intervention for this extremely anxious and depressed individual. His defenses were ineffective, and he would be incapable of functioning anywhere near his high level of intellectual ability without psychotherapeutic intervention.

In summary, the major aspects of the system presented depend on the interrelationship of the various Bender figures, as well as the interrelationship of the entire series of reproductions with other projective measures. The meanings engendered in the previous portions of this manual have been consistently confirmed throughout the years. The Bender provides a wealth of psychodynamic material that, in our opinion, has been greatly underutilized. The concept of covert pressures on an individual needs no emphasis by the authors, and clinicians familiar with any analytic approach should have no difficulty or reluctance in utilizing the preceding concepts. The need for clinical knowledge regarding the distortions on the Bender is of major importance if one is to become a competent professional clinician. Clinicians with eclectic or nonanalytic orientations should likewise find this interpretative system extremely useful. Earlier systems have been utilized by clinicians using a wide range of theoretical orientations. The present system is easily comprehended, and the psychodynamic symbolization is reasonably straightforward.

Plate 12.1
Interrelated Reproductions by a 15-year-old Male
(Reduced 50%)

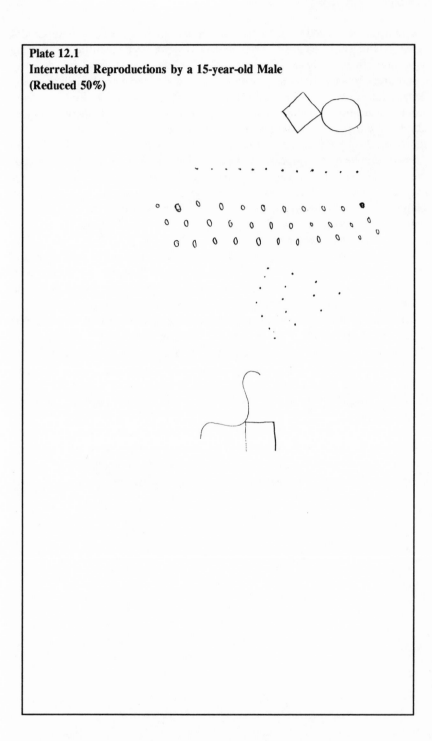

Plate 12.1 (continued)
Interrelated Reproductions
by a 15-year-old Male
(Reduced 50%)

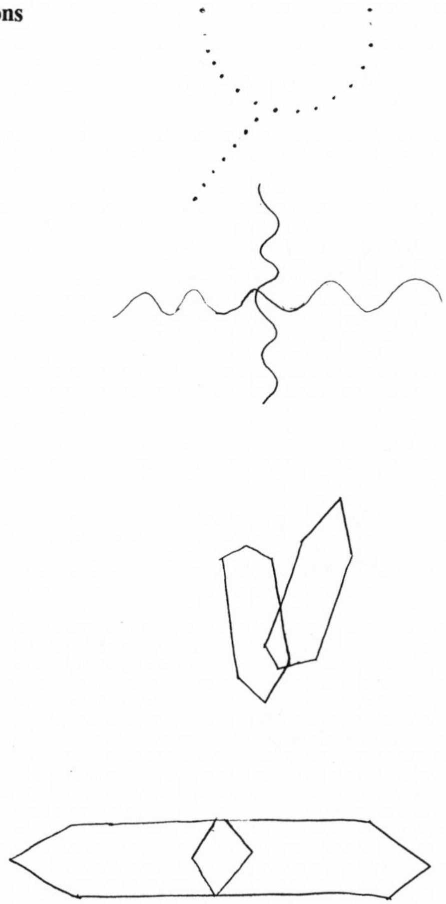

Plate 12.2a
Interrelated Reproductions by a 16.2-year-old Female
(Reduced 50%)

Plate 12.2a (continued)
Interrelated Reproductions by a 16.2-year-old Female
(Reduced 50%)

Plate 12.2b
Interrelated Reproductions by a 16.11-year-old Female
(Reduced 50%)

Plate 12.2b (continued)
Interrelated Reproductions by a 16.11-year-old Female
(Reduced 50%)

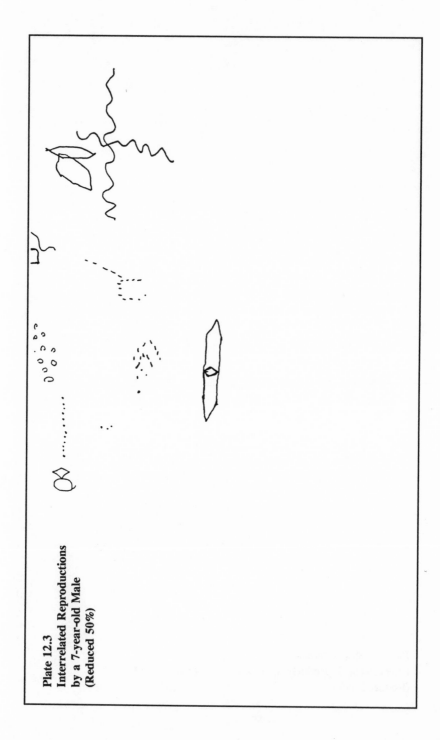

Plate 12.3
Interrelated Reproductions
by a 7-year-old Male
(Reduced 50%)

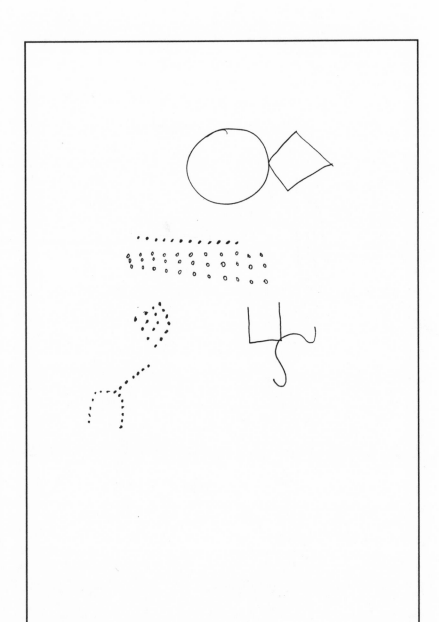

Plate 12.4
Interrelated Reproductions by a 37-year-old Male
(Reduced 50%)

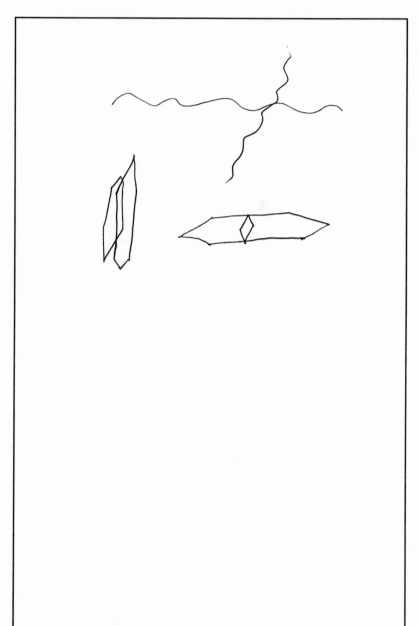

Plate 12.4 (continued)
Interrelated Reproductions by a 37-year-old Male
(Reduced 50%)

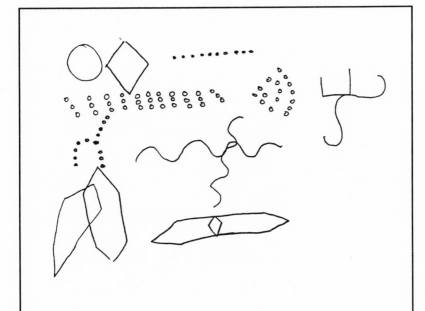

Plate 12.5
Interrelated Reproductions by a 30-year-old Female
(Reduced 50%)

Plate 12.6
Interrelated Reproductions by a 29-year-old Male
(Reduced 50%)

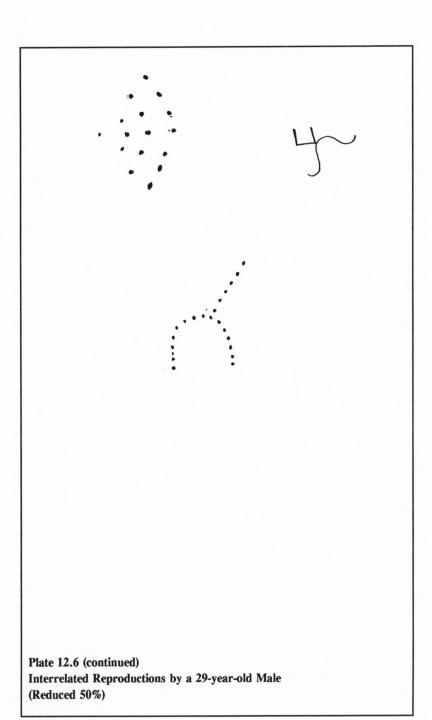

Plate 12.6 (continued)
Interrelated Reproductions by a 29-year-old Male
(Reduced 50%)

Plate 12.6 (continued)
Interrelated Reproductions by a 29-year-old Male
(Reduced 50%)

Plate 12.6 (continued)
Interrelated Reproductions by a 29-year-old Male
(Reduced 50%)

REVIEW QUESTIONS

1. Malingerers, pretending organic damage, are partially detectable by their

   a. disorientation.
   b. inconsistent patterns.
   c. diligence.
   d. none of the above.

2. The relationships among the reproductions of each design

   a. help assess malingerers.
   b. serve as cross-validating indices of suspected psychopathology.
   c. are useful for confirming neurologic impairment.
   d. all of the above.

3. Repeat reproductions of individual designs

   a. are too contaminated by practice effects to be of use.
   b. are most useful if conducted before the initial reproduction of the next design.
   c. can help rule out neurologic impairment.
   d. none of the above.

4. The placement of the designs at the right-hand side of the page, moving from right to left, reflects

   a. pedophiliac tendencies.
   b. overwhelming negativism.
   c. obsessive-compulsive tendencies.
   d. frontal lobe damage.

Chapter 13

RESEARCH

Scientific research in conceptual and abstract areas has been admirably conducted in every modern country for well over a century. Actuarial and projective test research in personality assessment has a long and full history. However, the BGT, like the Rorschach, "has often proved baffling to researchers and very irritating to those advocating the stringent application of psychometric principles to any psychological test" (Exner, 1986). Fortunately, projective tests like the BGT, the Rorschach, the HTP and others have been extensively studied and found to be valid, reliable and stable when administered appropriately by a professional specifically trained in their application and interpretation.

Over its life span there have been at least four major personality interpretative systems developed for the BGT, including those of Bender (1938), Hutt (1969), Koppitz (1963), and Pascal and Suttell (1951). Every one of these existing systems was primarily developed on theoretical approaches, and all lacked what today is considered adequate validity and reliability substantiation. Yet, as described earlier, this test is the third most widely used test in outpatient mental health centers (Piotrowski, 1985) and the most widely used in inpatient neuropsychological settings (Craig, 1979).

By now it should be understood that we are describing a new method of interpreting an existing set of stimuli reproductions. This is clearly not a new test per se, but as we see it, a work in progress that can be a powerful and desirable addition to any psychological test battery. Although Piotrowski's recent survey (1985) shows that the BGT is the third most widely used test in outpatient mental health settings--the Wechsler Adult Intelligence Scale (WAIS) was second, the MMPI first--many clinicians of all disciplines are unaware of its potential. For example, in "The Use of Projective Assessment by School Psychologists" (Vukovich, 1983), the BGT was frequently used, but not for assessment of personality or self-concept. This may be attributable in part to the fact that many clinicians are unaware of the validity of projective tests in personality assessment (Karon, 1978) and partly due to clinicians' unfamiliarity with validity studies conducted on the BGT as a personality measure for children and adults.

For example, the BGT was found to be a useful approach to brief screening for emotional disturbance in adolescents (Belter et al., 1989). Research by Edward Rossini and Joseph Kaspar (1987) suggests that the BGT, used according to Koppitz's method, possessed concurrent validity of emotional indicators for 7-to-10-year-olds assigned to three diagnostic groups: adjustment disorder, behavior disorder, and normal control, although the two clinical groups could not be differentiated. It appears as though this research would support the expanded use of the BGT as a personality measure in the nation's school systems.

The use of the BGT for assessment of personality was further studied by Hutt and Briskin (1960). They developed a nineteen-variable psychopathology scale and considered it useful for individuals 10 years of age and older. This was modified to 16 and older in a later study (Hutt and Miller, 1976). Interrater reliability for two experienced scorers on one hundred schizophrenic subjects was 96 percent (Hutt, 1969). A study of male delinquents in 1977 by three scorers yielded interrater reliability of 91 percent before treatment and 95 percent after forty weeks of therapy (Hutt and Dates, 1977).

David Schretlen and Hal Arkowitz (1990) investigated the accuracy with which a test battery including the Bender Gestalt Test could discern malingerers. They found that 92 to 95 percent of the subjects, consisting of prison inmates, noncriminal psychiatric patients, and mentally retarded males, were classified correctly.

Since the mid-1980s, nationally recognized projective test experts (Weiner, 1986; Blatt, 1986; Hertz, 1986) have begun to write about the limitations of actuarially based research. They have pointed to the need for exploration and development of conceptual research that would utilize appropriate psychometric techniques while addressing the need for the experimental and idiosyncratic test responses that purely actuarial research omits.

In 1986, Sidney Blatt, then president of the Society for Personality Assessment, described "a new, emerging conceptual-theoretical orientation in psychology...which places an emphasis...on the study of the individual's unique tendencies to construct meaning." Blatt's description was reiterated in 1986 by Weiner, another of the country's foremost authorities in personalty assessment. In his study, Weiner outlined a conceptual approach to the Rorschach Inkblots that is applicable to other perceptual tests, such as the BGT. He wrote, "In addition to considering how and what, the conceptually oriented clinicians will ask 'Why?'...By posing such questions, the conceptual approach takes Rorschach practitioners beyond the recognition of empirical relationships to the exploration of theoretical formulations of test and nontest behavior."

One of America's first and foremost Rorschach experts, Marguerite Hertz

(1986) in speaking about the future of Rorschach test research (clearly applicable to the BGT and other psychological measures), stated:

It has been demonstrated that the intuitive clinical process and the stylistic components of clinical judgement do lend themselves to investigation and that methods may be devised towards improving the accuracy of clinical judgement. It is my hope that we will devise similar research designs towards systematizing and communicating Rorschach ideology and skills. There is no reason why the qualitative features of a protocol, the cues utilized and the inferences made cannot be carefully defined, made explicit and transmitted to others, and used productively in practice and research ... It is now generally recognized that test scores and test patterns must be interrelated with contextual variables, and unless the nature of these interactions is considered, behavior cannot be described or predicted. In addition, the meaning and magnitude of any personality dimension gleaned from the Rorschach protocol cannot be made from numerical scores, patterns, clusters or formulas alone. (p. 408)

The present authors are well aware of the difficulties inherent in quantifying abstractions like personality traits with technique abstractions like multivariate statistical measures. Nonetheless, the validation and reliability of psychometric personality measures is a necessary challenge, despite the limitations.

Undoubtedly, reviewers and researchers will both accept and challenge our methodologic, theoretic, and statistical approaches. We welcome the interest, regardless of its intention or opinion. Karon's (1978) article, "Projective Tests are Valid," succinctly articulates our position. Simply, many studies of projective tests have found them valid and reliable, if the researcher utilizes appropriate statistical models and if the test interpreters possess relevant training and adequate experience. Our approach has been to employ experienced clinicians who have been in private practice an average of fifteen years.

To insure objectivity, our current system was evaluated independently by a research group led by Herbert M. Dandes, a professor at the University of Miami. The following is a synopsis of two studies completed at this writing. A complete description of these studies, as well as of four other studies underway at this time, is provided in Appendixes I through III. Once the four additional studies are completed, a clearer picture of the objectification, validity, and reliability of our system should be available.

Our initial study examined the validity of the Advanced Psychodiagnostic Interpretation (API) system. The present authors developed a 41-item rating scale that reflected the personality or developmental traits of subjects (Appendix II). A sample of eight psychologists and psychiatrists from the community were each asked to submit BGT protocols on two of their patients. These patients were selected by their therapists based on a thorough, in-depth psychodynamic understanding of their cases and on the availability of BGT protocols on them. Each therapist also completed the 41-item rating scale based on his or her total knowledge of the patient.

Five of the eight therapists returned completed materials. The present authors were then asked to fill out the same rating scales on these patients with only the BGT protocol, age, and gender of the individual. This practice, known as blind analysis, has a long and respectable history in personality assessment (Exner, 1986; Beck, 1960; Piotrowski, 1957 and 1965; Rapaport & Schafer, 1946; and Klopfer, 1954). Using Pearson Product-Moment Correlation Coefficients and comparing the therapists' ratings with their Bender interpretations, there was statistical significance beyond the .05 level on eight of the ten correlations. Six of the ten were above .50, suggesting favorable comparison with validity coefficients for many other widely used personality measures.

To establish the reliability of this system, four of the BGT protocols were randomly selected and submitted to each author separately. The present authors completed the same 41-item rating scale independently, and their interrater reliabilities were .86, .72, .68, and .65, all of which are statistically significant past the .005 level.

The second study examined teachability and subsequent interrater reliability. The authors developed a 112-item checklist of errors or "scorable indices," each having its own interpretative description (Appendix III). Each of these 112 items is linked to one or more of the 41-item rating scale. This scoring process was taught to five first-year doctoral students in one ninety-minute training session. The students were then separated and given one of two new BGT protocols, independently rating this protocol on both the 112-item and 41-item scales. The instructor/author then rated the same BGT protocols independently.

The student versus author ratings on the 112-item scale varied between 81 and 90 percent agreement. On the 41-item scale, the percentage of agreement varied between 80 and 93 percent. This clearly suggests that the API interpretative system can be quickly and efficiently taught and that high degrees of interrater reliability can be obtained.

Of course, as we have stated previously, these findings are not conclusive, and we do not in any way intend to create the impression that this is a new, "stand-alone" test. Our system, at best, will be a useful tool in the armamentarium of those who endeavor to assess abstractions like personality traits. We have found this system particularly useful as an initial "map" or guideline, to be corroborated by the balance of the psychological measures in a test battery. It is highly resistant to conscious, deliberate or accidental misrepresentation when used in this manner.

When one considers the argument for or against the "test battery" approach (Rapaport et al., 1945), it should be kept in mind that no one test has been able to correctly identify critical issues (i.e., suicide) more than about 75 percent of the time. In their 1977 "Suicide Constellation" with the Rorschach, John Exner and Joyce Wylie found that the Rorschach "correctly identified 44 of the 59 suicide cases (75%), while identifying 10 of the 50 depressives (20%), six of the schizophrenics (12%), and more of the nonpatients as false positives" (p. 346). Similarly, in the prediction of schizophrenia, they found 76 percent correct identifications of schizophrenia using a five-variable criterion. When only four variables were used, 87 percent were correctly identified, but 9 percent of the nonschizophrenics were incorrectly identified as schizophrenics (Exner 1981, 1983).

It is the professional responsibility of all who use tests to insure that individuals' traits are correctly identified as often as possible. While we clearly endorse the test-battery approach, we recognize that alternative approaches are both available and useful, if not limited.

The need for objective, unbiased research on projective tests by others is essential. It is neither helpful nor intellectually useful to negate projective tests as "unscientific." Given that no theoretical approach completely discerns the complexity of personality assessment, researchers must be willing to consider alternatives. Pan-theoretical, open-ended psychological measures like the BGT and Rorschach have clearly sustained the test of time and will, we believe, prove to be an invaluable aid in the assessment of a multitude of human traits for many years to come. The challenge for the twenty-first century will be the further refinement of conceptual research.

ANSWERS TO REVIEW QUESTIONS

CARD A:

1. d
2. c
3. d
4. c

CARD 1:

1. d
2. c
3. d
4. a

CARD 2:

1. c
2. d
3. c
4. d

CARD 3:

1. d
2. b
3. a
4. d

CARD 4:

1. b
2. a
3. c
4. b

CARD 5:

1. d
2. a
3. c
4. d

CARD 6:

1. b
2. c
3. a
4. c

CARD 7:

1. b
2. b
3. d
4. a

CARD 8:

1. d
2. c
3. d
4. a

INTERRELATIONSHIPS:

1. b
2. d
3. c
4. b

Appendix I

RESEARCH ON THE REICHENBERG-RAPHAEL INTERPRETIVE SYSTEM FOR THE BENDER GESTALT TEST

1. Preliminary study of the validity and interrater reliability of the Reichenberg and Raphael interpretive system: global interpretive statements versus clinician's judgement. Completed December 1990. (See Section 1.)

2. Teachability and interrater reliability of the Reichenberg-Raphael interpretive system. Completed March 1991. (See Section 2.)

3. Validity of the Reichenberg-Raphael interpretive system for the Bender Gestalt: interpretive statements versus clinician's judgment (item by item). In data collection phase. (See Section 3.)

4. Validity of the Reichenberg-Raphael interpretive system for the Bender Gestalt: normal versus pathological samples. Start date April 1, 1991. (See Section 4.)

5. Concurrent validity of the Reichenberg-Raphael interpretive system for the Bender Gestalt: interpretive statements versus MMPI. Start date April 1, 1991. (See section 4.)

6. Factor structure of the Reichenberg-Raphael interpretive system for the Bender Gestalt. Start date: April 1, 1991.

SUMMARY OF RESEARCH AS OF MARCH 8, 1991

The first study referenced above examined the validity and interrater reliability of this interpretive system. A global index of validity was obtained: the correlation between clinician's judgment on a 41-item rating scale (see Appendix II) versus the author's interpretive judgments on the same 41-item scale. Eight of the ten reliability coefficients were significant beyond the .05 level and six of the ten beyond the .005 level. The coefficients ranged from -.01 to .69. To determine interrater reliability, the two authors each independently rated four sets of drawings on the 41-item scale. The correlations between their ratings ranged from .65 to .86. Based on this study, the initial impression was that the system showed promise of being both reliable and valid, but more sophisticated research was needed.

The second study referenced above examined the teachability of the Reichenberg-Raphael system. The authors developed a 112-item list of "scorable points" on the Bender drawings (see Appendix III), each having its own interpretive statement and each being linked to one or more of the items on the 41-item rating scale. The results suggest that the interpretation rules are clear and that the system is easily teachable. The percentage of agreement between students and author on the 112-item scale ranged from 81 to 90 percent, and on the 41-item scale from 80 to 93 percent.

The third study, in progress, is a closer examination of the validity of this interpretive system. Bender drawings and 41-item checklists are being solicited from a national sample of psychologists. The validity of each of the 41 interpretive statements will be examined separately. Also, the relative validity of testing of more or less pathologically rated clients will be examined to determine whether there is an artifact caused by the prevalence rate of pathology in the sample.

The fourth study, which was to begin April 1, 1991, examines the ability of this system to distinguish between normal and pathological samples. "Normality" will be defined as having no clinical scales above 70 on the MMPI; pathology will be defined as having one or more clinical scales above 70.

The fifth study will examine the relationship between selected Reichenberg-Raphael (R-R) variables and MMPI scores. MMPI scales will be chosen which reasonably parallel R-R indices.

The sixth study will examine the factor structure of the R-R system. A sample of both undergraduate students and the archival files of Raphael and Reichenberg will be used for this study. The following analyses will be performed: (1) the factor structure of the 112-item scale will be examined to see whether it corresponds to the 41-item, logically derived scale; and (2) the 41-item scale will be factor analyzed to determine whether there are in fact 41 separate dimensions represented.

After the completion of these studies, we should have a firm knowledge of the reliability and validity of the Reichenberg-Raphael system. We will have examined the concurrent validity in three ways (R-R vs. clinician's judgment, R-R vs. MMPI, and ability to differentiate between normal and pathological samples). We will have examined the factor structure of the 112-item scale to see whether the items were correctly assigned to the 41-item scale, and we will have examined the factor structure of the 41-item scale to determine the independence of these items. We will also have established the "teachability" of the system, which requires clear and explicit interpretation rules. Further studies are being planned to examine the use of this system in specific populations.

SECTION 1: PRELIMINARY REPORT ON THE VALIDITY OF THE REICHENBERG-RAPHAEL INTERPRETIVE SYSTEM FOR THE BENDER VISUAL-MOTOR GESTALT DRAWINGS

Purpose: This study was designed to examine the validity of the Reichenberg-

Raphael system of interpreting Bender drawings. The authors designed this system to identify personality factors within a psychodynamic framework.

Method: The authors of this interpretive system (Reichenberg and Raphael) were asked to generate a list of interpretive statements that they believe could be drawn from Bender drawings. These statements were refined to eliminate redundancy and were then converted to a rating scale. This scale was submitted to an independent panel to review for clarity and gender neutrality, and revisions were made based on this review. All revisions were subject to approval by the authors of the system, to assure that the intent of each item was retained. The authors were then asked to specify the number of discriminations that could be made for each item, and the final rating scale was thus constructed. This scale consisted of 41 items, all of which reflect personality/developmental aspects of the subject. (See Appendix II.)

A sample of eight psychologists and psychiatrists from the local community was then identified. These therapists were all known to be familiar with psychodynamic constructs. The therapists were contacted by mail and were each asked to submit Bender drawings for two patients they had seen in therapy for at least one year. This criterion was used so that the therapists would select patients they knew well. They were then asked to fill out the rating scale for each patient based on their total knowledge of the patient and to send the drawings and the completed rating scales to the researcher.

Results: Of the eight therapists contacted, five returned the completed materials. There were then ten sets of Bender drawings and rating scales that served as the data base for this study.

Reliability: To establish the reliability of this interpretive system, four Bender drawings were randomly selected and were submitted to each author separately. The authors were asked to complete a rating scale for each of these subjects independently, and their completed rating scales were then examined for interrater reliability, using Pearson product-moment reliability coefficients. The interrater reliabilities for these four subjects were .86, .72, .68, and .65, all of which are significant well beyond the .005 level.

Validity: The six additional sets of Bender drawings were given to the first author (Raphael) for interpretation, and his rating scales for these subjects, plus his four rating scales used to establish reliability, were used to examine validity. These ten rating scales were correlated with the corresponding rating scales completed by the therapists. The results appear in Table 1.

As can be seen in Table 1, eight of the ten correlations between Bender interpretations and therapists' ratings were statistically significant beyond the .05 level. Six of the ten were above .50, comparing very favorably with validity coefficients for other personality measures.

Discussion: The present study was an initial investigation of a new method of interpreting Bender drawings with a psychodynamic framework. The first study was designed to determine whether, on initial inspection, this system is valid. The present evidence clearly suggests that this is a valid system. While this study was based on a small sample and looked at the validity of each subject separately, it served the purpose of giving first empirical evidence of the validity of this system.

One can observe in Table 1 that there was a lack of significant correlation between therapist judgment and Bender interpretation in two of the ten subjects. These two sets of data will be subjected to closer analysis to find the reason for this lack of correlation.

Future Research: A second study is now underway that will provide more detailed analysis of the validity of the Reichenberg-Raphael interpretive system. In this study, 100 psychologists have been selected from the membership of the Division of Psychoanalysis of the American Psychological Association. The purpose of the study was explained, and the psychologists were asked about their willingness to each submit one set of Bender drawings for a patient they have seen in therapy for at least one year. A minimum number of forty psychologists will be accepted, and if necessary the original list of one hundred will be augmented by random selection until the forty volunteers are obtained. They will each be asked to submit one set of Bender drawings and to fill out the rating scale. With this greater number of subjects we will be able to (1) Examine validity item by item, with many cases for each item, (2) Decide whether sampling from a "pathological" population spuriously inflates the validity, and (3) Examine whether modifying the rating scale can increase interrater reliability.

Table 1
Pearson Product-Moment Correlation Coefficients:
Bender Interpretations versus Therapists' Ratings

Subject	r	p
1	.58	< .005*
2	.61	< .006
3	.59	< .005
4	-.01	NS
5	.26	< .05
6	.62	< .006
7	/00	NS
8	.52	< .005
9	.39	< .005
10	.60	< .005

*All probabilities reported are one-tailed.

SECTION 2: TEACHABILITY AND INTERRATER RELIABILITY OF THE REICHENBERG-RAPHAEL INTERPRETIVE SYSTEM FOR THE BENDER GESTALT

This study examined the teachability of the Reichenberg-Raphael system. The authors developed a 112-item list of "scorable points" on the Bender drawings (see Appendix III), each having its own interpretive statement. Each of these 112 statements was also linked to one or more of the items on the 41-item rating scale. A group of five doctoral students was taught this system in approximately 90 minutes, during which time they practiced using it on two sets of drawings. They were then given one of two research Bender drawings, not previously seen by the author/instructor, and independently rated this Bender on both the 112-item and 41-item scale. Following the training, and without seeing the students' responses, the author/instructor rated the same two Benders on both rating scales. The students' ratings were compared with the author's ratings and yielded the results shown in Tables 2 and 3.

Summary: The results indicate (1) that the system can be easily taught and (2) that a high degree of interrater reliability can be obtained. It is interesting to note that a higher degree of interrater reliability was obtained on the 41-item scale than on the 112-item scale. This is probably due to the redundancy in the 41-item scale: most items contain more than one reference to the 112-item scale, and the scoring of each item is determined by clear interpretation rules. At the current time, the 112-item scale is being examined to see which items caused the most difficulty for the students, and these items will be revised for further clarity.

Table 2
Students versus Author on 112-Item Scale

Drawing No.	Percentage of Agreement
1	89
1	90
2	82
2	81
2	85

Table 3
Students versus Author on 41-Item Scale

Drawings No.	Percentage of Agreement
1	93
1	88
2	88
2	88
2	80

SECTION 3: UNIVERSITY OF MIAMI HUMAN RESEARCH PROTOCOL FORM, BEHAVIORAL SCIENCES SUBCOMMITTEE

1. Title of Project: Assessing the validity of a psychodynamically based interpretive system for the Bender Visual-Motor Gestalt Test.

2. Principal Investigator and Collaborators: Principal Investigator: Herbert M. Dandes, Ph.D. Collaborators: Janine Osborne, Doug Reichel, Stephen Gill.

3. Performance Site(s): Approval from the site is required before initiation of the study. Attach a copy of the letter or submit a copy of the letter when available. Institution: University of Miami.

4. Proposed Start Date: March 1, 1991.

5. Funding Agency: Not applicable.

6. Project Objectives: The study is designed to assess the validity of a new, psychodynamically based interpretive system for the Bender Visual-Motor Gestalt Test. The author of the new interpretive system will give blind interpretations of forty Bender Visual-Motor Gestalt drawings taken from archival records provided by clinicians. These interpretations will be statistically compared to the clinical profiles of the patients provided by the clinicians in order to assess the validity of the new interpretive system.

7. Recruitment Procedure: Mailout or handout requests.

8. Methods and Procedures: From the membership of Division 39 of the American Psychological Association, 100 psychologists will be randomly selected. From those who respond, 40 participants will be selected. Each psychologist will select one patient, over the age of 16, whom the psychologist has seen in therapy for at least one year. A Bender Visual-Motor Gestalt Test will be obtained for each patient. Further, the psychologist will complete a 41-item checklist based on his or her total knowledge of the patient. The Bender drawings and clinical checklist will be mailed to the researchers and be anonymously coded for confidentiality. The drawings will then be interpreted by the

author of the new interpretive system. Based on the interpretation, the author will also fill out the 41-item checklist. Standard statistical analysis will be done to compare the interpreter's checklist with the psychologist's checklist for the same patient.

SECTION 4: UNIVERSITY OF MIAMI HUMAN RESEARCH PROTOCOL FORM, BEHAVIORAL SCIENCES SUBCOMMITTEE

1. Title of Project: Validity of the Reichenberg-Raphael Interpretive System for the Bender-Gestalt Drawings II.
2. Principal Investigator and Collaborators: Herbert M. Dandes, P.I.; Janine Osborne, Doug Reichel, Stephen Gill.
3. Performance Site(s): Institution: University of Miami.
4. Proposed Start Date: April 1, 1991.
5. Funding Agency: Not applicable.
6. Project Objectives: The purpose of this project is to continue studying the validity of the Reichenberg-Raphael interpretive system for the Bender-Gestalt drawings. Specifically, this study will (1.) examine whether this system can differentiate between normal and pathological subjects and (2.) Determine the relationship between this system and a standardized paper-and-pencil personality inventory.
7. Recruitment Procedure: Psychology subject pool sign-up sheets.
8. Methods and Procedures: Two sources of subjects will be used: the psychology subject pool and the archival records of Reichenberg and Raphael. For the first group of subjects, the MMPI-2 and Bender Visual-Motor Gestalt Test will be administered. The subjects will be divided into two groups: those scoring above T-score of 70 on at least one clinical scale and those not scoring above 70 on any clinical scale. Benders will be administered to all subjects, and these two groups will be compared to determine whether the R-R system can distinguish between them. For the second source of subjects, Benders and MMPIs will be obtained. Subjects will be identified who score above 70 on at least one clinical scale, and this group will be compared with the college student "normals" to see whether they can be distinguished by their R-R Bender scores.

Both groups of subjects will be combined for the next analysis, which will examine the relationship between R-R interpretive statements and MMPI-scale scores.

9. Subject Population: University of Miami.
10. Records: Subject records regarding this protocol will be maintained in the files of the principal investigator of this project and in the files of Reichenberg and Raphael.
11. Confidentiality: Data will be recorded with special code numbers, and there will be no link between that code and the subject's identity.
12. Deceptive Techniques: Not applicable.
13. Investigator's Evaluation of Potential Physical, Psychological or Social Risk to Subjects: No risk.
14. Informed Consent: To be signed by each participant or parent.

15. Debriefing: Subjects will not be debriefed.

16. Medical Facet: This research does not have any medical facet.

17. Assurances: I affirm that no change will be made in the methods of procedure or the informed consent statement of this study without prior approval of the reviewing committee.

I affirm that the principal investigator will prepare a summary of the project annually, including all information specified by the "Guidelines for Behavioral Research" involving Human Subjects at the University of Miami.

I affirm that I have received a copy of the above guidelines, and I agree to follow and abide by them.

Herbert M. Dandes
Principal Investigator

Appendix II

THE REICHENBERG-RAPHAEL
41-ITEM RATING SCALE

1. Interparental intimacy

    1) cohesive, close, loving
    2) present but not exaggerated
    3) alienated, divisive, separated
    4) not applicable

2. Interparental aggression

    1) peaceful, nurturing, tranquil
    2) present but not exaggerated
    3) violent, abusive, combative, sadistic
    4) not applicable

3. Potential for being abused (including past abuse)

    1) safe, unharmed, unscathed
    2) present but not exaggerated
    3) abused, violated, victimized
    4) not applicable

4. Psychological parent

    1) mother figure
    2) neither/both
    3) father figure
    4) not applicable

5. Inconsistency of mother figure

   1) incongruent, divergent, discrepant
   2) present but not exaggerated
   3) congruent, united, cohesive
   4) not applicable

6. Inconsistency of father figure

   1) incongruent, divergent, discrepant
   2) present but not exaggerated
   3) congruent, united, cohesive
   4) not applicable

7. Lack of nurturance by mother figure

   1) neglect, ignore, not care for
   2) present but not exaggerated
   3) nourish, care for, provide for maintenance, sustenance
   4) not applicable

8. Lack of nurturance by father figure

   1) neglect, ignore, not care for
   2) present but not exaggerated
   3) nourish, care for, provide for maintenance, sustenance
   4) not applicable

9. Sexually traumatized

   1) secure, safe, unharmed sexually
   2) present but not exaggerated
   3) molestation, sodomy, sexually abused
   4) not applicable

10. Inability to control impulses

   1) prudent, cautious, circumspect, judicious
   2) present but not exaggerated
   3) imprudent, careless, rash, capricious
   4) not applicable

11. Chronicity of impulse control deficits (throughout one's lifetime)

1) acute, temporary, casual, transient
2) present but not exaggerated
3) longstanding, chronic, deep-rooted, prolonged
4) not applicable

12. Depression (as a trait)

1) happy, cheery, content, absence of depression
2) present but not exaggerated
3) sad, desolate, dejected, dispirited, lethargic, sorrowful, melancholic
4) not applicable

13. Psychosis

1) coherent, organized thoughts and behavior, good reality testing
2) present but not exaggerated
3) incoherence, emotional turmoil, gross distortion of thoughts or poor reality testing
4) not applicable

14. Regression (as a trait)

1) mature, stable, evolving, capable
2) present but not exaggerated
3) revert, relapse, become childish or infantile
4) not applicable

15. Acting out sexually

1) monogamous, devoted, loyal
2) present but not exaggerated
3) promiscuity, prostitution, lewd, libertine, philander, polygamous
4) not applicable

16. Paranoia

1) trusting, open, easygoing
2) present but not exaggerated
3) mistrustful, overly suspicious, persecutory, guarded
4) not applicable

17. Dependency

1) independent, self-sufficient, decisive, responsible
2) present but not exaggerated

3) passive, subordinated, lacks self-confidence, indecisive
4) not applicable

18. Dissociation

1) clear-thinking, alert, perceptive
2) present but not exaggerated
3) cognitive disorganization, psychogenic amnesia, loss of one's own reality
4) not applicable

19. Propensity toward addiction

1) mature, independent, self-confident
2) present but not exaggerated
3) dependent, impulsive, immature, poor self-esteem, compulsive
4) not applicable

20. Lack of conformity to rules and regulations

1) dishonest, untrustworthy, disobedient
2) present but not exaggerated
3) obedient, trustworthy, honest
4) not applicable

21. Ideational turmoil

1) organized, stable, clear thinking
2) present but not exaggerated
3) psychotic, disorganized thinking, hallucinating
4) not applicable

22. Anger proneness

1) calm, relaxed, tolerant
2) present but not exaggerated
3) violent, explosive, combative, volatile
4) not applicable

23. Conflicts with authority figures

1) dutiful, obedient, law abiding
2) present but not exaggerated
3) rebellious, antisocial, insolent, sadistic, defiant, lawless
4) not applicable

24. Degree of affect drivenness

    1) logical, controlled, cogent, goal-directed, rational
    2) present but not exaggerated
    3) labile, hysterical, impulsive
    4) not applicable

25. Self-denigration

    1) self-respecting, dignity, pride
    2) present but not exaggerated
    3) self-loathing, self-punitive, poor self-concept, dislike of self, masochistic
    4) not applicable

26. Sado-masochism (confusion between sex and aggression)

    1) kind, gentle, benevolent
    2) present but not exaggerated
    3) cruelty, malice, sexual perversion or aberration
    4) not applicable

27. Inadequacy of separation from parental figures

    1) symbiosis, inadequacy, immaturity, dependent
    2) present but not exaggerated
    3) autonomy, maturity, self-sufficiency
    4) not applicable

28. Perception of gender dominance

    1) gender specificity, acceptance of one's gender
    2) present but not exaggerated
    3) repudiation of one's anatomic sex, gender identity crisis, discontent with one's gender
    4) not applicable

29. Controlling/manipulative tendencies

    1) honest, accepting, cooperative
    2) present but not exaggerated
    3) domineering, authoritarian, directive to others for one's own benefit or satisfaction
    4) not applicable

30. Psychopathy (as a trait)

    1) honest, law-abiding, socially conforming
    2) present but not exaggerated
    3) sadistic, vicious, antisocial, violent, impulsive, unlawful, dishonest
    4) not applicable

31. Impotence

    1) competence, qualified, skilled, capable of performing sexually
    2) present but not exaggerated
    3) powerlessness, inability to perform sexually or otherwise inept
    4) not applicable

32. Passivity

    1) active, directive, decisive
    2) present but not exaggerated
    3) inactive, inert, receptive, indifferent
    4) not applicable

33. Borderline traits

    1) organized, stable personal relationships, self-confident, self-respecting, law-abiding
    2) present but not exaggerated
    3) impulsivity, pattern of unstable personal relationships, identity disturbance, marked mood shifts, self-punitive acts, unlawful
    4) not applicable

34. Intrapunitive tendencies

    1) self-protective, self-respecting
    2) present but not exaggerated
    3) self-destructive, suicidal, self-denigration
    4) not applicable

35. Repression

    1) permit, accept, allow, tolerate
    2) present but not exaggerated
    3) constrain, hinder, denial, suppress, restrain
    4) not applicable

36. Hysterical/histrionic

    1) calm, stable, objective, rational

2) present but not exaggerated
3) self-centered, over-reactive, vain, dependent, impulsive
4) not applicable

37. Organic impairment

   1) normal, functional and healthy
   2) present but not exaggerated
   3) brain damage, neurologic impairment, minimal cerebral dysfunction
   4) not applicable

38. Psychosexual immaturity

   1) developed, mature
   2) present but not exaggerated
   3) childlike, sophomoric, incomplete, prepubescent
   4) not applicable

39. Penetration anxiety

   1) enjoyment of intercourse, pursuit of sexual relations
   2) present but not exaggerated
   3) fear of harm to genital area, fear of intercourse, (females) vaginismus, sexual anhedonia
   4) not applicable

40) Castration anxiety

   1) enjoyment of intercourse, pursuit of sexual relations
   2) present but not exaggerated
   3) sexual avoidance, fear of intercourse, impotence, sexual anhedonia
   4) not applicable

41. Sexual preoccupation

   1) sexually mature, sexually healthy
   2) present but not exaggerated
   3) sexual compulsions, excessive sexual behavior with sexual or nonsexual objects
   4) not applicable

Appendix III

THE REICHENBERG-RAPHAEL
112-ITEM SCORING INSTRUMENT

COMMON DESIGN DISTORTIONS

1. Any of the nine designs comes close to (within a 1/4") any edge of the paper.
   Interpretation: patient needs/seeks environmental limits in the areas the particular design(s) measure; sociopathy, psychopathy.
   Scale ratings: 10-3, 11-3, 15-2, 19-3, 20-3, 23-3, 24-2, 30-3, 33-3, 38-3.
2. Any drawing goes off any edge of the paper.
   Interpretation: psychosis.
   Scale ratings: 10-3, 11-3, 13-3, 21-3, 30-3.
3. All of the designs are drawn in the upper third of the paper.
   Interpretation: artificial impulse control, sociopathy, acting out pressures, defective egos.
   Scale ratings: 10-3, 11-3, 15-3, 19-3, 20-3, 21-3, 22-3, 23-3, 24-3, 26-3, 29-3, 30-3, 33-3, 34-3, 38-3, 41-3.
4. Designs are drawn along the right side of the paper.
   Interpretation: extremely negativistic, rebellious, sociopathic.
   Scale ratings: 10-3, 11-3, 13-2, 15-2, 16-2, 19-2, 20-3, 21-2, 22-3, 23-3, 26-3, 29-3, 30-3, 38-3.
5. Any collision(s) or near collision(s) between 2 or more designs.
   Interpretation: severe pathology with an emphasis on areas the colliding designs measure, some form of psychosis, schizophrenia.
   Scale ratings: 10-3, 11-3, 13-2 (if near collision(s)) or 13-3 (if actual collision(s)), 15-2, 19-3, 20-3, 23-3, 24-2, 30-3, 33-3, 38-3.

CARD A

6. Circle drawn higher than square.
   Interpretation: female/mother figure dominant, psychological parent figure.
   Scale rating: 4-1.

7. Square drawn higher than circle.
   Interpretation: male/father figure dominant, psychological parent figure.
   Scale rating: 4-3.

8. Circle, square height even.
   Interpretation: neither/both dominant, psychological parent figure.
   Scale rating: 4-2.

9. Figures touch as per model.
   Interpretation: interparental intimacy.
   Scale rating: 1-1.

10. Square penetrates circle.
    Interpretation: interparental aggression, verbal and/or physical abuse.
    Scale ratings: 2-3, 3-3.

11. Either figure appears to be pulling away.
    Interpretation: interparental intimacy strained.
    Scale rating: 1-2.

12. Figures do not touch at all (separated).
    Interpretation: separated, uninvolved parental figures.
    Scale rating: 1-3.

13. Incomplete circle (i.e. overlapping lines, incomplete, broken lines, projecting lines, ending lines that do not meet).
    Interpretation: deficient nurture by the female/mother figure.
    Scale ratings: 5-3, 7-3.

14. Incomplete square (same as above).
    Interpretation: deficient nurture by the male/father figure.
    Scale ratings: 6-3, 8-3.

15. Circle has line projecting at bottom (tail).
    Interpretation: castrating,, domineering female/mother figure.
    Scale ratings: 2-3, 3-2, 22-3, 26-2, 34-2, 40-3.

16. Exaggeratedly sharp points on square.
    Interpretation: accentuated hostility from male/father figure.
    Scale ratings: 2-3, 3-2, 22-3, 23-3, 26-2, 34-2, 29-3, 40-2.

17. Card A drawn in the middle of the page, subsequent designs below it.
    Interpretation: adult patients only: excessive dependency on/ importance of parental figures.
    Scale ratings: 17-3, 23-3, 27-3.

18. Card A drawn in the middle of the page, subsequent designs above and to its sides.
    Interpretation: adult patients only: overwhelming turmoil involving parental figures.
    Scale ratings: 13-2, 17-3, 19-3, 23-3, 27-3, 33-3.

19. Line quality fluctuates (dark to light, vice-versa) within the circle.
    Interpretation: female/mother figure inconsistent.
    Scale rating: 5-3.

20. Line quality fluctuates (dark to light, vice-versa) within the square.
    Interpretation: male/father figure inconsistent.
    Scale rating: 6-3.

21. Entire circle drawn darker than the square (square drawn appropriately).
    Interpretation: intensified hostility to and from the female/mother figure.
    Scale ratings: 2-2, 22-2, 26-2, 29-2, 34-2.

22. Entire square drawn darker than the circle (circle drawn appropriately).

Interpretation: intensified hostility to and from the male/father figure.
Scale ratings: 2-2, 22-2, 26-2, 29-2, 34-2.
23. Inability to draw diamond.
Interpretation: brain damage, minimal cerebral dysfunction.
Scale ratings: 37-3.

CARD 1

24. Fewer than 12 dots.
Interpretation: tenuous impulse control.
Scale ratings: 10-3, 11-2, 15-2, 19-2, 20-2, 22-2, 23-2, 24-2, 30-2, 33-2, 36-2, 38-2.
25. More than 12 dots.
Interpretation: preoccupation with control.
Scale ratings: 10-1, 16-2, 20-1, 21-2, 22-2, 23-2, 24-1, 29-3, 34-2, 35-2, 38-2, 41-2.
26. Extreme extension of the line of dots across the page.
Interpretation: psychotic preoccupation with control.
Scale ratings: 10-3, 11-3, 13-3, 14-3, 15-2, 21-3, 24-3, 41-3.
27. Downward slope of line of dots.
Interpretation: ongoing depression.
Scale ratings: 10-2, 12-3
28. Upward slope of line of dots.
Interpretation: acting-out potential.
Scale ratings: 10-3, 11-3, 15-2, 19-2, 20-3, 23-3, 24-3, 30-2, 33-2, 36-2, 38-2.
29. Variability in the slope of the line of dots (wavy line).
Interpretation: fluctuating impulse control.
Scale ratings: 10-2, 11-2, 15-2, 19-2, 20-3, 23-2, 24-2, 30-2, 33-2, 36-2, 38-2.
30. Regression from dots to circles.
Interpretation: regression in affective functioning, excessive dependency needs, presence of intense anger.
Scale ratings: 10-3, 11-3, 12-3, 14-3, 17-3, 19-2, 20-2, 21-2, 22-3, 23-2, 24-3, 27-2 33-3, 36-2, 38-2.
31. Dots are drawn in pairs.
Interpretation: obsessive-compulsive and paranoid pressures.
Scale ratings: 13-2, 16-3.
32. Disproportionately large gaps or spaces between dots.
Interpretation: dissociation.
Scale ratings: 3-2, 9-2, 18-2 (if one gap) or 18-3 (more than one).
33. Inconsistent line quality (some heavy, some light).
Interpretation: tenuous impulse control.
Scale ratings: 10-2, 11-2, 20-2, 23-2, 24-2, 33-2, 36-2, 38-2.
34. Excessive line quality (heavy, dark lines).
Interpretation: accentuated anger and rage over having to control impulses.
Scale ratings: 10-2, 11-2, 20-2, 22-2, 23-2, 24-2, 35-2.
35. Insufficient line quality (light, faint lines).
Interpretation: passive, reluctant, withholding of emotions, submissive.
Scale ratings: 10-1, 17-3, 25-2, 32-3, 36-2.

CARD 2

36. Downward slope of line of circles.
    Interpretation: conscious dissatisfaction with self.
    Scale ratings: 12-3, 25-3, 34-2.
37. Upward slope of line of circles.
    Interpretation: volatile, temperamental, overt, exaggerated expression of affect.
    Scale ratings: 10-2, 11-2, 22-3, 23-2, 24-3, 33-2, 36-3.
38. Columns of circles lose their angulation.
    Interpretation: intense conscious depression.
    Scale rating: 12-3.
39. First attempt (ascending) erased and redrawn straight.
    Interpretation: ability to self-correct acting-out behavior.
    Scale ratings: 10-2, 11-1, 22-2, 23-2, 24-2, 36-2.
40. First attempt (ascending) crossed out and redrawn straight.
    Interpretation: self-dissatisfaction, ongoing depression.
    Scale ratings: 12-3, 25-3, 34-3.
41. Disproprtionately large gaps or spaces between dots.
    Interpretation: dissociation.
    Scale ratings: 3-2, 9-2, 18-2 (1 gap) or 18-3 (more than 1 gap).
42. Any circles closed and colored in.
    Interpretation: pronounced anger.
    Scale ratings: 22-3, 34-2.
43. Any vertical column of three circles has an additional fourth circle.
    Interpretation: acute schizophrenic processes.
    Scale ratings: 13-3, 14-3, 21-3.
44. Extreme angulation in the columns of circles.
    Interpretation: intense conscious self-dissatisfaction, intense depression, ideational turmoil.
    Scale ratings: 12-3, 13-3, 14-2, 21-3, 25-3, 34-3.
45. Circle(s) larger than the model.
    Interpretation: exaggerated dependency.
    Scale ratings: 17-3, 19-3, 25-2, 27-3, 31-2.
46. Any circles touch each other.
    Interpretation: exaggerated dependency, exaggerated anger and emotional turmoil.
    Scale ratings: 17-3, 19-3, 21-2, 22-3, 24-3, 25-2, 27-3, 31-2, 33-2, 36-2.

CARD 3

47. Female patients only: regression from dots to circles.
    Interpretation: dislike of men and sexual intercourse, anger at father.
    Scale ratings: 9-2, 13-2, 23-3, 28-2, 31-2, 36-2, 39-3.
48. Female patients only: design erased and made smaller.
    Interpretation: pathological concerns and fears regarding penetration.
    Scale ratings: 9-3, 28-2, 31-2, 36-2, 39-3.
49. Male patients only: regression from dots to circles.
    Interpretation: enraged, often towards father, ideational turmoil and subsequent

regression, incapable of separating sexual and aggressive drives.
Scale ratings: 9-2, 13-2, 14-3, 15-3, 17-2, 21-3, 22-3, 23-3, 24-2, 26-3, 27-2, 28-2, 30-2, 31-2, 38-3, 40-3, 41-2.

50. Male patients only: design erased and made smaller.
Interpretation: not adequately separated from mother, intense concerns regarding potency.
Scale ratings: 17-3, 23-2, 25-2, 27-3, 28-3, 31-3, 32-3, 38-3, 40-3, 41-2.

51. Drawing has more than sixteen dots.
Interpretation: hostility and anger in terms of sexual functioning.
Scale ratings: 15-3, 22-3, 24-2, 26-3, 28-2, 38-2, 39-2, 40-2, 41-2.

52. Drawing has less than sixteen dots.
Interpretation: denial and rejection of sexual aggression.
Scale ratings: 22-2, 24-2, 26-2, 38-2, 39-2, 40-2.

53. Either more or less than seven dots in longest line (seven-dot line at back of arrow).
Interpretation: anger that is hidden and denied at conscious levels.
Scale ratings: 22-2, 24-2.

54. Significant space (especially between front and back of arrow) between line of dots.
Interpretation: intense, covert rage reaction denied once controls are reinstituted.
Scale ratings: 10-3, 11-1, 13-3, 21-3, 22-3, 24-3, 30-3.

55. Center row of dots not straight.
Interpretation: possible organic impairment.
Scale ratings: 37-2.

CARD 4

56. Female patients only: box and curve line overlap.
Interpretation: dislikes men, prone to controlling or verbally/physically abusing them, identity confusion, self-loathing, identification with aggressive father.
Scale ratings: 2-3, 3-2, 4-3, 10-2, 11-2, 15-2, 20-2, 22-3, 23-3, 24-2, 26-3, 27-2, 28-3, 29-3, 31-3, 33-3, 34-3, 36-3, 38-3, 39-3, 41-2.

57. Female patients only: curved line under or partially under the horizontal line of the box.
Interpretation: pseudoseductive, sexually dysfunctional, accentuates femininity, passivity.
Scale ratings: 17-3, 23-1, 25-3, 26-2, 27-3, 31-3, 32-3, 33-3, 34-3, 35-1, 36-3, 38-3.

58. Female patients only: curved line drawn nearer to the right vertical side of the box.
Interpretation: intense anger, intensely competitive with and mistrustful of other women.
Scale ratings: 10-1, 16-2, 18-1, 22-3.

59. Female patients only: pencil line darker on this design, as well as on Card A.
Interpretation: intense anger, inability to maintain subordinate role.
Scale ratings: 16-2, 17-1, 20-3, 22-3, 23-3, 25-2, 26-2 29-3, 32-1, 33-2, 34-2, 36-2.

60. Female patients only: rounded angles on box.
Interpretation: feminization or denigration of men.
Scale ratings: 8-2, 19-2, 23-2, 26-2, 29-2.

61. Female patients only: curved line drawn substantially larger than model.
Interpretation: female/mother figure dominant sex; domineering.

Scale ratings: 4-1, 7-1, 17-1, 28-1, 29-3, 32-1.
62. Female patients only: Box drawn substantially larger than the model.
    Interpretation: male/father figure dominant sex; subservient.
    Scale ratings: 4-3, 8-1, 17-3, 23-1, 25-2, 27-2, 28-1, 32-2, 34-2.
63. Male patients only: curved line overlaps box.
    Interpretation: perceives women as threatening, dominated by females.
    Scale ratings: 3-2, 17-3, 23-3, 25-2, 27-3, 28-2, 31-3, 38-3, 40-3.
64. Male patients only: box penetrates curved line.
    OR
65. Right vertical side of box is higher than left.
    OR
66. Curved line is under horizontal line of box.
    OR
67. Box line quality is darker than curved line.
    OR
68. Curved line drawn substantially larger than the model.
    OR
69. Box drawn substantially larger than the model.
    Interpretation: dislikes women, seeks to verbally or physically hurt them, uses pseudomasculine, "macho" image with women, deeply identity confused with a manifest need to prove their masculinity in accentuated ways, promiscuous and homophobic.
    Scale ratings: 10-2, 11-2, 15-2, 22-2, 26-2, 28-2, 29-2, 30-2, 31-2, 38-3, 41-3.
70. Any separation between figures.
    Interpretation: severe peer relationship disturbances, mistrustful, paranoid, addiction-proneness.
    Scale ratings: 16-3, 17-2, 19-2.
71. Either or both side(s) of the box tilt inward.
    Interpretation: constricted, emotionally ungiving male/father figure.
    Scale ratings: 8-3, 17-3, 19-3, 22-3, 23-3, 27-3.
72. Either or both side(s) of the curved shape tilt inward.
    Interpretation: constricted, emotionally ungiving female/mother figure.
    Scale ratings: 7-3, 17-3, 19-3, 22-3, 23-3, 27-3.

CARD 5

73. Female patients only: design has less than seven dots on straight row (penis symbol).
    Interpretation: penetration anxiety, sado-masochistic, castrating, masculine woman.
    Scale ratings: 3-2, 9-2, 22-2, 26-2, 28-3, 29-2, 31-2, 36-2, 38-2.
74. Male patients only: design has less than seven dots on straight row (penis symbol).
    Interpretation: ineffectual, passive, impotent, lacks self-esteem.
    Scale ratings: 9-2, 17-3, 20-2, 23-1, 25-3, 28-3, 31-3, 32-3, 33-2, 38-2, 40-3.
75. First dot on left of semicircle is missing (and/or semicircle is lopsided - giving the appearance that the first dot is missing).
    Interpretation: inadequate bonding with/nurturance from mother in the first year of life; schizophrenia and/or manic depressive psychosis.
    Scale ratings: 7-3, 13-2, 14-2, 17-3, 19-3, 21-2, 27-2, 38-3.

76. Any excessive separation(s) between dots on semicircle.
    Interpretation: separation from mother, exacerbated and traumatic.
    Scale rating: 7-3.
77. Any regression from dots to circles (including on any previous, erased attempts at this design).
    Interpretation: exacerbated dependency processes and excessive demand for nurture due to nurture deprivation; psychotic, psychopathic, addition-proneness.
    Scale ratings: 7-3, 8-3, 13-2, 14-3, 15-3, 17-3, 18-2, 19-3, 21-3, 22-3, 24-3, 27-3, 28-2, 30-2, 33-3, 36-3, 38-3.
78. Any deviation from the intersection of breast/penis symbols between the eleventh and twelfth dots (left to right).
    Interpretation: Trouble with the onset of puberty, possibility of sexual trauma including molestation.
    Scale ratings: 9-3, 15-2, 26-2, 27-2, 31-2, 38-2, 39-2, 40-2.
79. Dashes instead of dots used for either or both figures.
    Interpretation: exaggerated dependency, sexual avoidance, anorexia.
    Scale ratings: 17-3, 19-3, 28-3, 31-3, 38-3, 39-3, 40-3.
80. Any significant rotation of the design.
    Interpretation: distorted, deviant dependency needs, affective turmoil.
    Scale ratings: 7-3, 8-3, 12-3, 13-3, 14-3, 17-3, 19-3, 22-3, 24-3, 27-3, 30-3, 33-3, 36-3, 38-3.

CARD 6

81. Vertical line intersects horizontal line to the right of center and below it (out and down).
    Interpretation: severe depression, psychotic processes, schizophrenia.
    Scale ratings: 12-3, 13-3, 14-3, 21-3.
82. Vertical line intersects horizontal line to the right of center and above it (out and up).
    Interpretation: weakened superego, defective ego, acting out, affective turmoil, character disordered (possibly in psychotic proportions).
    Scale ratings: 10-3, 11-3, 13-2, 14-2, 15-3, 19-3, 20-3, 23-3, 24-3, 26-3, 30-3, 33-3, 38-3, 41-3.
83. Vertical line intersects horizontal line to the left of center and below it (in and down).
    Interpretation: exaggerated use of repression regarding sex or hostility; forgetfulness, histrionic, hysterical.
    Scale ratings: 18-2, 35-3, 36-3, 38-3.
84. Vertical line intersects horizontal line to the left of center and above it (in and up).
    Interpretation: depression, intra-punitive, suicidal, homicidal, acting out.
    Scale ratings: 12-3, 22-3, 25-3, 26-3, 34-3.
85. Sharp upswing of the horizontal line.
    Interpretation: acting out, affective turmoil.
    Scale ratings: 10-3, 11-3, 12-3, 19-3, 21-2, 24-3, 27-3, 33-3, 36-3, 38-3.
86. Sharp downswing of the horizontal line.
    Interpretation: exaggerated, dysphoric tendencies.
    Scale ratings: 12-3, 24-2, 34-2.
87. Horizontal line lighter than vertical line.

Interpretation: suppression of affect.
Scale ratings: 10-1, 16-2, 24-2, 29-2, 35-3.
88. Horizontal line darker than the vertical line.
Interpretation: affect driven.
Scale ratings: 10-2, 11-2, 12-2, 22-2, 36-3.
89. Pointed curves on either or both lines.
Interpretation: possible organic impairment.
Scale rating: 37-2.
90. Any erasures on the horizontal line.
Interpretation: accentuated affect, affective turmoil.
Scale ratings: 10-3, 11-3, 12-3, 13-2, 24-3, 33-3, 36-3.
91. Any erasures on the vertical line.
Interpretation: accentuated hostility.
Scale ratings: 10-3, 11-3, 12-2, 20-2, 22-3, 23-3, 24-3, 26-3, 29-2, 30-3, 33-3, 34-2.

CARD 7

92. Any broken lines, flattening of figures, rounding of points or loss of angulation.
Interpretation: possible organic impairment.
Scale rating: 37-2.
93. Any broken lines.
Interpretation: sexual aversion, disruption of sexual ideation into consciousness and/or disruption in sexual functioning.
Scale ratings: 9-2, 15-2, 26-2, 31-2, 38-2, 39-3, 40-3.
94. Figures do not overlap (at all or insufficiently).
Interpretation: castration anxiety in males, overwhelming sexual fear for either sex.
Scale ratings: 9-2, 31-2, 38-3, 39-3,40-3.
95. Figures overlap excessively.
Interpretation: preoccupation with libidinal ideation, possibility of primary process (schizophrenia).
Scale ratings: 10-3, 13-3, 15-3, 21-3, 38-3, 41-3.
96. Figures drawn significantly smaller or larger than the model.
Interpretation: sexual functioning and/or sexual ideation is seen as threatening, intense sexual pressures, sexual acting out.
Scale ratings: 10-3, 11-1, 13-3, 38-3, 39-3, 40-3, 41-3.
97. Any erasure(s).
Interpretation: penetration anxiety by either sex.
Scale ratings: 3-2, 36-2, 38-3, 39-3.
98. Excessive erasure(s) (either or both figures completely erased).
Interpretation: gross sexual turmoil; psychosis.
Scale ratings: 13-3, 14-3, 14-3, 21-3, 24-3, 26-3, 30-3, 31-3, 36-3, 38-3, 39-3, 40-3.
99. Design drawn on a separate page.
Interpretation: intense anxiety generated by sexual nature of this design; psychosexual immaturity; avoidance of sexual ideations.
Scale ratings: 9-3, 31-3, 32-3, 38-3, 39-3, 40-3.
100. Any faint lines.
Interpretation: sexual avoidance, feelings of sexual inadequacy, immaturity,

prepubescent psychosexual fixation.

Scale ratings: 9-2, 15-2, 28-2, 31-2, 32-2, 36-2, 38-3, 39-3, 40-3.

101. Darkened lines and/or darkened, extra-sharp points.

Interpretation: aggressive and/or sadistic tendencies, sex and aggression merged, possible sexual trauma, sexual battery.

Scale ratings: 9-2, 15-3, 22-3, 26-3, 30-3, 31-2, 38-3, 41-3.

102. Inconsistent line quality (dark and faint lines).

Interpretation: sexual trauma.

Scale rating: 9-3.

CARD 8

103. Female patients only: outer shape drawn smaller than the model.

Interpretation: conscious dislike of heterosexual activity and/or gender identity disturbance.

Scale ratings: 9-2, 28-2, 36-2, 38-3, 39-3.

104. Female patients only: center diamond extends beyond the lines of the outer shape.

Interpretation: fear of heterosexual behavior or sexual anhedonia.

Scale ratings: 3-3, 9-3, 15-2, 26-2, 28-3, 31-3, 38-3, 39-3.

105. Male patients only: outer shape drawn significantly smaller than the model.

Interpretation: sexual inadequacy, dysfunctional concerns.

Scale ratings: 9-2, 28-2, 31-3, 38-3, 40-3.

106. Any broken lines.

Interpretation: serious sexual turmoil including confusion of sex and aggression, possible sexual trauma.

Scale ratings: 3-2, 9-3, 13-2, 14-3, 26-3, 28-2, 31-2, 38-3, 39-3, 40-3, 41-3.

107. Design drawn larger than the model.

Interpretation: sexual preoccupation, possible schizophrenic processes.

Scale ratings: 13-2, 14-3, 15-3, 21-3, 38-3, 41-3.

108. Wavy, curved lines in outer shape.

Interpretation: low frustration tolerance, self-denigration.

Scale ratings: 10-2, 11-2, 12-2, 22-2, 24-2, 25-3, 34-3, 36-2.

109. Lengthening of the outer symbol.

Interpretation: disturbing ideational turmoil, severe aggressive ideation involving sexual functioning.

Scale ratings: 3-2, 9-2, 10-2, 13-2 15-2 21-3, 24-2, 26-2 33-3, 38-3, 41-3.

110. Any faint lines.

Interpretation: penetration anxiety, fear of intercourse.

Scale ratings: 3-3, 9-3, 15-2, 26-2, 28-3, 31-3, 38-3, 39-3, 40-3.

111. Any heavy shading of lines, darkened or exaggerated points.

Interpretation: merger of sex and aggression, serious sexual turmoil, possible sexual trauma.

Scale ratings: 3-2, 9-3, 13-2, 14-3, 26-3, 28-2, 31-2, 38-3, 39-3, 40-3, 41-3.

112. Any broken lines and/or rounded corners.

Interpretation: possible organic impairment.

Scale rating: 37-2.

References

Atkinson, L., Quarrington, B., Alp, I. E., and Cyr, J. J. 1986. "Rorschach Validity: An Empirical Approach to the Literature." *Journal of Clinical Psychology, 42,* 360-62.

Beck, S. J. 1937a. "Introduction to the Rorschach Method: A Manual of Personality Study." *American Orthopsychiatric Association Research Monographs, no. 1.* New York: American Orthopsychiatric Association.

Beck, S. J. 1960. *The Rorschach Experiment.* New York: Grune & Stratton.

Belter, R. W., McIntosh, J. A., Finch, A. J., Williams, L. D. et al. 1989. "The Bender Gestalt as a Method of Personality Assessment With Adolescents." *Journal of Clinical Psychology, 45,* 414-23.

Bender, L. 1938. "A Visual Motor Test and Its Clinical Use." *American Orthopsychiatric Association Research Monographs, no. 3.* New York: American Orthopsychiatric Association.

Binet, A. and Henri, V. 1895. "La psychologie individuelle." *L'Annee Psychologique, 2,* 411-65.

Blatt, S. J. 1986. "Where Have We Been and Where Are We Going? Reflection on 50 Years of Personality Assessment." *Journal of Personality Assessment, 50(3),* 343-46.

Cattell, J. M. 1887. "Experiments on The Association of Ideas." *Mind, 12,* 68-74.

Cohen, R., Montague, P., Nathanson, L. and Swerdlik, M. 1988. *Psychological Testing.* California: Mayfield Publishing Co.

Craig, P. J. 1979. "Neuropsychological Assessment in Public Psychiatric Hospitals: The Current State of The Practice." *Clinical-Neuropsychology, 1(4),* 1-7.

Dana, R. H. 1978. "Rorschach." In O. Buros, *The Eighth Mental Measurements Yearbook* (pp. 1040-42). Highland Park, N.J.: Gryphon Press.

Exner, J. E. 1981. "The Response Process and Diagnostic Efficacy." 10th International Rorschach Congress, Washington, D.C.

Exner, J. E. 1983. "Rorschach Assessment." In I. B. Weiner (Ed.), *Clinical Methods in Psychology* (2nd ed.). New York: Wiley.

Exner, J. E. 1986. *The Rorschach: A Comprehensive System Volume 1: Basic Foundations.* 2nd ed. New York: Wiley.

Exner, J. E. and Wylie, J. 1977. "Some Rorschach Data Concerning Suicide." *Journal of Personality Assessment, 41,* 339-48.

Frank, L. K. 1939. "Projective Methods For The Study of Personality." *Journal of Psychology, 8,* 389-413.

Freud, S. 1912-13. *Totem and Taboo.* Translated. New York: Moffatt, Yard, 1919.

Galton, F. 1883. *Inquiries Into Human Faculty and Its Development.* London: Macmillan.

Hain, J. D. 1964. "The Bender Gestalt Test: A Scoring Method for Identifying Brain Damage." *Journal of Consulting Psychology, 28,* 473-78.

Haramis, S. L. and Wagner, E. E. 1980. "Differentiation Between Acting-Out and Non-Acting-Out Alcoholics With The Rorschach and Hand Test." *Journal of Clinical Psychology, 36(3),* 791-97.

Hertz, M. 1986. "Rorschachbound: A 50-year Memoir." *Journal of Personality Assessment, 50(3),* 396-416.

Hutt, M. L. 1969a. *The Hutt Adaptation of The Bender Gestalt Test.* 2nd ed. New York: Grune and Stratton.

Hutt, M. L., Miller, L. J. 1975. "Further Studies of a Measure of Adience-Abience: Reliability." *Journal of Personality Assessment, 39(2),* 123-28.

Hutt, M. L. and Dates, B. G. 1977. "Reliabilities and Interrelationships of Two HABGT Scales for a Male Delinquent Population." *Journal of Personality Assessment, 41,* 492-96.

Jensen, A. R. 1965. "Review of the Rorschach." In O. Buros (ed.), *The Sixth Mental Measurements Yearbook* Highland Park, N.J.: Gryphon Press.

Karon, B. P. 1978. "Projective Tests are Valid." *American Psychologist, 33(8),* 764-65.

Klopfer, B., Ainsworth, M., Klopfer, W. and Holt, R. R. 1954. *Developments in the Rorschach Technique: Vol 1. Technique and Theory.* Yonkers-on-Hudson, NY: World.

Koppitz, E. M. 1963. *The Bender Gestalt Test for Young Children.* New York: Grune and Stratton.

Koppitz, E. M. 1975. *The Bender Gestalt Test for Young Children, Vol II: Research and Application.* New York: Grune and Stratton.

Kraepelin, E. 1892. *Uber die Beeinflussung Einfacher Psychischer Vorgange Durch Eininge Arzneimittle.* Jena: Fischer.

Lacks, P. 1984. *Bender Gestalt Screening for Brain Dysfunction.* New York: Wiley.

McClelland, D. C. 1981. "Is Personality Consistent?" in A. I. Rabin, J. Aronoff, A. M. Barclay and R. H. Zucker (eds.), *Further Explorations in Personality.* (pp. 87-113). New York: Wiley.

Pascal, G. R., and Suttell, B. J. 1951. *The Bender Gestalt Test.* New York: Grune and Stratton.

Paulker, J. D. 1976. "A Quick Scoring System For The Bender Gestalt: Interrater Reliability and Scoring Validity." *Journal of Clinical Psychology,* 86-9.

Piotrowski, C., Sherry, D, and Keller, J. W. 1985. "Psychodiagnostic Test Usage: A Survey of The Society for Personality Assessment." *Journal of Personality Assessment, 49,* 115-19.

Piotrowski, Z. A. 1957. *Perceptanalysis.* New York: Macmillan.

Piotrowski, Z. A. 1965. "Computer Imitation of Man." *American Journal of Clinical Hypnosis, 8(1),* 3-7.

Rapaport, D., Gill, M. M., and Schafer, R. 1945-1946. *Diagnostic Psychological Testing.* Chicago: Year Book Publishers.

Ritzler, B. and Alter, B. 1986. "Psychodiagnostic Testing in APA Approved Clinical

Psychology Programs." *Professional Psychology: Research and Practice, 15(3),* 450-56.

Rossini, E. D. and Kaspar, J. C. 1987. "The Validity of The Bender Gestalt Emotional Indicators." *Journal of Personality Assessment, 51(2),* 254-61.

Rorschach, H. 1921. *Psychodiagnostics.* New York: Grune and Stratton.

Schilder, P. 1934. "Space, Time and Perception." *Psyche, 14,* 124.

Schretlen, D. and Arkowitz, H. 1990. "A Psychological Test Battery to Detect Prison Inmates Who are Faking Insanity or Mental Retardation." *Behavioral Science and the Law, 8,* 75-84.

Schulberg, H. and Tolor, A. 1961. "The Use of The Bender Gestalt Test in Clinical Practice." *Journal of Projective Techniques, 25,* 347-51.

Spearman, C. 1926. *The Abilities of Man: Their Nature and Measurement.* New York: Macmillan.

Tenopyr, M. L. and Oeltjen, P. D. 1981. "Personnel Selection and Classification." In M. R. Rosenzweig and L.W. Porter (eds.), *AnnualReview of Psychology.* California: Annual Review.

Tolor, A., and Schulberg, H. 1963. *An Evaluation of The Bender Gestalt Test.* Springfield, Ill: Charles C. Thomas.

Ulrich, L. and Trumbo, D. 1965. "The Selection Interview Since 1949." *Psychological Bulletin, 63(2),* 100-16.

Vukovich, D. H. 1983. "The Use of Projective Assessment by School Psychologists." *School Psychology Review, 12(3),* 358-64.

Weiner, I. B. 1977. "Approaches to Rorschach Validation." In M.A. Rickers-Ovisankina (ed.), *Rorschach Psychology,* (pp. 575-608).

Weiner, I. B. 1986. "Conceptual and Empirical Perspectives on the Rorschach Assessment of Psychopathology." *Journal of Personality Assessment, 50(3),* 472-79.

Wertheimer, M. 1923. "Studies in The Theory of Gestalt Psychology." *Psychologische, Forschung, 4,* 301-50.

Index

Acting-out, 9, 12, 19, 20, 27, 28, 35, 36, 45, 63, 84, 95

Actuarial research, 114

Adjustment disorder, 114

Administration of the Bender,
  directions, 8
  environmental factors, 10
  group, 4
  sequence and tempo, 7
  settings, 10, 113
  time limit, 9

Adolescence, 21, 83, 84, 93, 95, 96

Affect, 18, 21, 27, 61-64, 72, 84, 93-96

Affective functioning, 19, 62, 64

Affective turmoil, 63

Aggravated assault, 36, 45

Aggression, 8, 12, 35, 36, 42, 45, 73, 83, 84, 95

Alter, Barbara, 4

Anger, 9, 12, 20, 21, 26, 27, 33, 35, 36, 43-45, 52, 53, 61, 63, 64, 73, 81, 90, 92

Angulation, 27, 28

Antisocial behavior, 27

Anxiety, 8, 9, 42, 45, 52, 60, 73, 74, 81, 92

Aphasia, 3

API (Advanced Psychodiagnostic Interpretation of the BGT), 115, 116

Arson, 36, 96

Artificial constriction, 12

Beck, Samuel J., 2, 116

Behavior disorder, 114

Behavioral turmoil, 21

Bender, Lauretta, 2, 3, 6-7, 92, 113

Bender Gestalt Test, 2-8, 92, 114
  use with children, 3, 11, 36, 73, 114

Blatt, Sidney, 114

Blind analysis, 44, 116

Bonding, 51, 95

Brain damage, 3

Bulimia, 60, 72

Castration anxiety, 52, 73, 74, 95

Cohen, Ronald, 3, 4

Collisions, 21, 28, 36, 52, 53, 63, 92, 96

Compulsivity, 72

Computerization, 4

Conceptual validation, 5

Constriction, 12, 36, 62, 96

Control line, 21, 94

Cost containment, 3, 6

Counting the dots, 9

Craig, Paul, 3, 4, 113

Culture-free testing, 4

Dandes, Herb, 115

Defenses, 20, 93, 97

Denial, 28, 35, 63, 83

ABOUT THE AUTHORS

Dr. NORMAN REICHENBERG has served as a court-appointed expert witness in local, state and federal courts for over twenty-five years and is considered a pre-eminent expert in the field of psychological testing. He served as Chief of Psychology at Jackson Memorial Hospital in Miami, Florida, for ten years before entering private practice, specializing exclusively in psychological evaluations on a referral-only basis.

Dr. ALAN J. RAPHAEL began his career as a consulting psychologist for the University of Miami School of Medicine. In 1982 he entered full-time private practice, specializing in psychological evaluations, psychotherapy for children and adults, and industrial consultation. He is an Adjunct Associate Professor at the University of Miami, teaching Rorschach Interpretation. He is regularly called upon to serve as a court-appointed expert.

Over the past thirty years, the authors have evaluated over twenty thousand individuals in virtually every setting, including in-patient psychiatric and general medical/surgical units, outpatient mental health clinics, private practice, and federal, state, and local penal institutions. Together they have established Reichenberg & Raphael Review, Incorporated, a company specializing in psychological testing and scoring and the review of psychological materials.